WASHINGTON COUNTY
CHRONICLES

WASHINGTON COUNTY
CHRONICLES

Historic Tales from Southwestern Pennsylvania

HARRIET BRANTON

FOREWORD *by* A. PARKER BURROUGHS
EDITED *by* EMSIE AND LESLIE PARKER

THE
History
PRESS

Published by The History Press
Charleston, SC 29403
www.historypress.net

First published 2013

Manufactured in the United States

ISBN 978.1.60949.869.6

Library of Congress CIP data applied for.

To Clarence

CONTENTS

CONTENTS

FOREWORD

The southwestern corner of Pennsylvania was once at the edge of the frontier. Though its story often begins with the gritty pioneers who put down roots here and the Native Americans who resisted them, its human history is much older. The archaeological excavation at Washington County's Meadowcroft Rockshelter has shown that people have wandered these rolling hills for at least sixteen thousand years.

Three comprehensive histories of Washington County have been written, roughly a generation apart, first by Boyd Crumrine in 1882, then by Joseph McFarland in 1910 and Earle R. Forrest in 1926. Although no newer volume has been published since that time, the region's intriguing past has hardly been neglected.

Harriet Branton's series of essays, written in the 1980s and published in the *Observer-Reporter* of Washington, opened a window though which readers could view local history with sparkling clarity. Her writings, painstakingly researched and composed in plain-spoken prose of wit and precision, engendered a new interest in the county's hardscrabble beginnings, its revolt against federal authority with the Whiskey Rebellion, its position on both the National Road and the Underground Railroad, its mineral wealth and exploitation, its immigrants, heroes and villains.

In this book, which arranges Branton's essays chronologically, are stories important well beyond the borders of this region, like that of Solomon Spaulding, who may have been the true author of the Book of Mormon. Joseph Smith, founder of the Latter-day Saints movement, claimed the book was written on gold tablets and handed to him by an angel, but many of Spaulding's friends and relatives claim their local storyteller was the creator of the unpublished text, which disappeared from a Pittsburgh printer's shop in the early nineteenth century. Spaulding spent the last years of his life and is buried in Amity, but the controversy lives on.

There are tales here of rebels, innovators and artistic pioneers. David Bradford led the Whiskey Rebellion, the first test of the power of the new federal government of President Washington; F. Julius LeMoyne built the first crematorium; and Rebecca Harding Davis, with works of realistic fiction like *Life in the Iron Mills*, stirred the national conscience.

Branton's glimpses into local history are not all about the famous and significant, however. Many of these essays celebrate ordinary people in extraordinary circumstances: the quick, the quirky and quixotic.

These are stories about how this corner of Pennsylvania grew to what it is and, in a larger sense, what made America what it is today.

—A. Parker Burroughs

Parker Burroughs, writer and painter, spent forty-one years in the newspaper business. He is the editor of *200 Years: Our History Through the Pages of the Observer-Reporter* and author of *Enter, With Torches: Recollections of a Grumpy Old Editor.*

Preface

Washington County, Pennsylvania, which in 1981 celebrated its two hundredth birthday, had been the domain of the white man for not much longer than that. Until the middle of the eighteenth century, it was a region inhabited by a relatively small number of Indians, mostly of the Delaware and Shawanese tribes. The unhappy Delawares, who were originally from eastern Pennsylvania, had been relentlessly pushed westward by the bullying tactics of the Iroquois Confederation, which controlled the territory between the Alleghenies and the Ohio River. The Shawanese had emigrated northward from their homeland in southeastern North America. These tribes had no fixed homes, and the only permanent Indian settlement in what is now Washington County was a hunting camp on Catfish Creek that was occasionally frequented by the famous Delaware chief, Tingoocqua. The Indians' few contacts with whites came mostly from the German, English and French traders who penetrated the wilderness west of the Alleghenies.

Until 1760, there were no settlements of white men, lawful or unlawful, west of the Monongahela and east of the Ohio. The region between the rivers was a wilderness with no meadows or plains, where oak, maple, hickory, ash, walnut, cherry, chestnut and pine trees grew in profusion. The land was covered with a dense thicket of undergrowth that at intervals even reached all the way across its numerous streams. The forest was indeed so wild that Indian trails, so narrow that they allowed groups to travel only in single file, followed the ridges of the highlands, where the land was dry and clear enough to permit their passage.

Washington and Gist (with Scout)—1753, by Malcolm Parcell. Famed explorer Christopher Gist accompanied George Washington on his missions to French forts in southwestern Pennsylvania. *Courtesy Dr. E. Ronald Salvitti.*

This untamed wilderness, traversed by many streams, among them Mingo, Ten Mile, Chartiers, Raccoon and Buffalo Creeks, nevertheless held promise for grazing lands and fertile soil well suited to almost any kind of farming. And underneath it all were vast resources of coal, petroleum and natural gas.

But in the middle of the eighteenth century, the future Washington County was really the province of the Iroquois, and they proposed to keep it that way. The colonial governments of Virginia and Pennsylvania cooperated; they tried to keep His Majesty's subjects from straying across the mountains and settling in the lush forbidden lands of the Iroquois Confederation (which at that time included the "Six Nations" of the Mohawks, Oneidas, Onondagas, Cayugas, Senecas and Tuscaroras.) After the French and Indian War, the government of Pennsylvania even went so far as to decree the death penalty for those who insisted on defying the law and settling beyond the Monongahela River. It was all in vain. Settlers crossed the Alleghenies, put down roots and went in for farming in a big way. They intended to stay. The Indians protested vigorously, complaining bitterly that their hunting grounds were being ruined.

In 1767 and 1768, more governmental proclamations against settlement were issued; councils were held, during which representatives of both sides delivered impassioned speeches, but all efforts to evict the determined settlers met with failure. Finally on November 5, 1768, by the terms of the Treaty of Fort Stanwix, the Iroquois Confederation sold to the proprietary government of Pennsylvania all of the land that included the present counties of Westmoreland, Fayette, Greene, Washington and those parts of Allegheny and Beaver Counties that lay south of the Ohio River. In no time, the trickle of settlers became a steady stream.

While the Indians may have surrendered title to the region, the Virginians did not. Virginia insisted that most of southwestern Pennsylvania belonged to it and even named it West Augusta. A Virginia court was actually convened near the present city of Washington in September 1776. The heated quarrel dragged on for years and occasionally threatened to blossom into a full-scale war. Finally, both Virginia and Pennsylvania appointed members to serve on a commission to examine the controversy, settle the boundary question and resolve claims of settlers who had bought land in Pennsylvania under Virginia patents. The complicated and acrimonious dispute was at last settled without bloodshed in the fall of 1780, just six months before the establishment of Washington County on March 28, 1781.

ACKNOWLEDGEMENTS

M uch like the proverbial child raised by a village, this volume could not have come to fruition without the generous help of many people. It all began with a newspaper blessed with an editor who understood the importance of educating the community about its heritage. Gratitude is extended to Park Burroughs for his unstinting enthusiasm and time spent exhuming photos used in the paper more than a quarter century ago. Clayton Kilgore of the Washington County Historical Society believed in the endeavor from the beginning. Without his many hours spent scanning old newsprint, this project would still be embryonic.

Illustrations add depth to any story, and relevant historical images are not always easy to find. Thanks are given to Amy Welch, Washington & Jefferson College (W&J) archivist; Professors Jennifer Harding and Linda Troost, W&J College; Ella Hatfield, Citizens Library; Suzanne Wylie, former Waynesburg University librarian; Dr. James Randolph, Waynesburg University; Ruth Craft, Cornerstone Genealogical Society, Waynesburg; Duncan and Miller Glass Museum; and Bethel Presbyterian Church.

Washington County is proud of several nationally known artists who found inspiration in our past. Our gratitude to Dr. E. Ronald Salvitti, who graciously made available his exceptional collection of Malcolm Parcell paintings, and to Mark Marietta, who took all of the Parcell and Duncan and Miller Glass Museum photographs and also captured landmark images. We are greatly indebted to gifted artist Ray W. Forquer of Countryside Prints, Inc. for permission to use his work and to Peter West of Peter West

Galleries for gathering, photographing and scanning the Forquer paintings. Judith O'Toole, Westmoreland Museum of American Art, Greensburg, courteously provided us with the work of J. Howard Iams.

Special thanks to our ever helpful editor at The History Press, Hannah Cassilly, who made it all happen and, of course, to our families and countless friends who listened—mostly patiently—while our conversational range seemed limited to the progress of *Washington County Chronicles*. Every one of you played a part.

—Harriet Branton
—Emsie and Leslie Parker

INTRODUCTION

The essays in this book were written some thirty years ago as part of a series of historical features published in the *Washington Observer-Reporter*. They were designed to commemorate the bicentennials of both the establishment of Washington County, Pennsylvania, in March 1781, and the log school in Canonsburg the same year to which Washington and Jefferson (W&J) College traces its beginning.

The essays were not intended to provide histories of either the county or W&J College. Rather they were written as a series of vignettes, or footnotes, to history—sidebar stories about people and events that were not quite important enough to be recorded in a formal history of either but that are appealing in their own right.

Last year, through the efforts of my good friends and editors, Emsie and Leslie Parker, a plan to reprint a small collection of some of these essays was presented to the editors at The History Press. The editors liked the idea, so here we have stories about people and events that helped to shape the development of western Pennsylvania from an uncharted wilderness to the interesting and vibrant society that it is today.

—Harriet Branton

Nineteenth-century map of Washington County. *Courtesy Washington and Jefferson College.*

The Five Courts of
Washington County

The present Washington County courthouse—the fourth to be built
here—is really the fifth court to serve citizens of this region. It was in
the fall of 1776, even before the formation of Washington County, that the
first English-speaking court west of the Alleghenies was in session. It met on
September 17 in Augusta Town (the present Gabby Heights area).

At that time, Washington County was part of the territory in dispute
between Virginia and Pennsylvania. The region was called West Augusta
and, as such, was claimed by Virginia as part of Augusta County. The
complicated and sometimes acrimonious dispute was finally settled through
the expedient of extending the Mason-Dixon line westward.

Washington County was created by act of the Pennsylvania legislature
on March 28, 1781. The first terms of court for the newly created county
were held in David Hoge's log house, which stood at approximately the
intersection of Main Street and Strawberry Avenue. Until 1787, court was
held in various houses, including those of Charles Dodd and James Wilson,
who collected rental fees ranging from six to sixty pounds for the privilege.

In October 1781, land for a public square was purchased from David
Hoge for the purpose of erecting a courthouse. The lot, 240 feet square,
fronted on Monongahela Street (now Main), between Ohio Street (now
Beau) and Johnson Alley (now Cherry Avenue). For this parcel of land,
Hoge received five shillings. For some unknown reason, the county trustees
dragged their feet in getting construction underway for a "courthouse and
gaol [jail]" and were roundly scolded by the court, through the prothonotary.

The *Court Minutes of April Term 1782* reminded the trustees of the urgent necessity for a courthouse and warned that "the Court will find themselves under the disagreeable necessity of representing the remissness of the said Trustees, if something is not speedily done in that respect."

Something was finally done, although not very speedily. The rebuke from the court resulted in the beginning of construction in 1783 but work proceeded so slowly that the building was not ready for occupancy until July 1787. In the meantime, according to historian Earle Forrest, county prisoners were housed in Charles Dodd's log stable, which had been "fitted up and strengthened for the purpose." The temporary arrangement was not very secure and resulted in frequent complaints from the court, the sheriff and others. Once, when some particularly unruly criminals were confined there, it was necessary to get help from the militia to guard them.

At last, after four years of effort, a single log building, two stories high, was completed. The first floor housed the courthouse and jail, and the second was used as the first quarters for Washington Academy. The total cost of construction was $3,115.56. The structure was apparently unsatisfactory from the moment of its occupancy. The jail proved to be about as secure as Dodd's stable, for prisoners were always escaping. The building had a short life, however. It burned to the ground during the winter of 1790–91. The court went back to John Wilson's house, and the Washington Academy was left homeless.

The second courthouse was two stories high, constructed of brick for $8,000 and was ready for occupancy in July 1794. It fronted Main Street and was topped by a tower with a cupola, a weather vane and an arrow. In the tower was a bell that was rung to summon the citizenry to court or for a fire alarm. It was also used to toll for funeral processions.

Included in the public square by this time were several other buildings that housed various county offices. This complex was enhanced in 1824 by the construction of a somewhat medieval prison built of limestone; the first floor walls were four feet thick. The building was surrounded by a stone wall fifteen feet high and four feet thick. This jail was in use for about forty years and cost $3,500.

This second courthouse required thousands of dollars in continuing repairs and alterations, and in 1836, citizens were summoned to a public meeting to consider the advisability of constructing yet another courthouse. After much discussion, resolutions were passed that stated the need for a new building and recommended that the question be put to the voters in the spring. This was done, and the voters defeated the proposal soundly.

There the matter rested until the spring of 1839, when the sorry state of the courthouse was referred to a grand jury for consideration. That body studied the commissioner's report that stated $5,000 would be needed to repair the old structure, and $12,000 would be required to build a new one. The jury declared the old building unfit for use and recommended construction of a new courthouse.

Bids for courthouse number three were advertised in June 1839; contracts were awarded in July, and work began immediately. The old building was demolished, and temporary quarters were again rented. The new structure was completed in the fall of 1842 at a cost of $24,958—about double the original estimate.

A statue of George Washington that adorned the top of the building was the object of a curious lawsuit. James P. Millard was retained to produce a statue. When it was completed, the commissioners refused to accept delivery on the grounds that Millard had not fulfilled the terms of his contract. Millard sued the commissioners for $257.00. The case came up for trial in August 1843, and the jury found for the plaintiff in the amount of $132.00, with costs of $152.87½.

A curious lawn ornament! Purchased by Charles Hallam after the third courthouse was demolished in 1898, it stood on his lawn at the corner of Hallam and Locust Avenues for many years. *Courtesy* Washington Observer-Reporter.

The commissioners had offered to settle for the sum of eighty dollars, but Millard turned down the deal. Not only did he win his case, but he also won commendation from the jury for fulfillment of the contract and a job well done. The Millard statue made history for another reason. Local boys found it great sport to roam through the courthouse. They especially liked to climb through the trapdoor onto the roof of the dome and stand beside the statue. Some even succeeded in sitting on its shoulders. One particularly daring lad managed on one occasion to stand on its shoulders with his hands behind his head. Startled passersby gawked in horror as he made his way down safely. That boy grew up to operate a print shop on South Main Street.

The radiant dome soars above the rotunda, divided into twelve sections of stained glass converging in a rose skylight. The Roman arches reflect the building's classical, Italian Renaissance style. *From* The People's Palace.

When the third courthouse was torn down in 1898, the controversial statue was sold to Charles Hallam, who placed it on a pedestal in front of his home at the corner of Highland and Locust Avenues. There it stood as a familiar landmark for many years.

In 1867, the commissioners contracted to spend about $50,000 for the construction of a new prison and additional space for the courthouse.

The original terra cotta statue of George Washington suffered three lightning strikes between 1900 and 1917. The last strike decapitated the figure, and it was removed from the dome. In 1927, the courthouse received a new $12,000 bronze statue, still in place today. *Courtesy* Washington Observer-Reporter.

These structures served for about thirty years. As time went by, the third courthouse was not large enough for the voluminous county business; offices were crowded, and the basement was filled with valuable documents. The commissioners won the approval of the judges to erect still another courthouse and jail complex. Bids were advertised, contracts were let and construction began in the spring of 1898. The estimated cost was $425,000.00.

THE PEOPLE'S
Palace

The Washington County Courthouse
Washington, Pennsylvania

Washington County Courthouse—The People's Palace. "Well may the people be proud of this noble, massive building." *Washington Observer,* 1900. *Courtesy Michael Ray Photography.*

Again some citizens resisted; 372 people signed a petition protesting the project. However, the court refused to intervene, and the construction proceeded. Additions and changes pushed the final cost to $934,027.45. This included decorating and furnishings, a jail plus cells and other expenses. The grand new fireproof building, constructed in Italian Renaissance style with a statue of George Washington crowning the dome as before, was dedicated with appropriate public ceremony on November 17, 1900.

The new statue of Washington, eighteen feet tall and made of terra cotta, also had adventures. It was struck by lightning three times. First the nose and then the chin had to be repaired; the third strike resulted in the loss of the head entirely. The statue was removed in 1917, and it was not until 1927 that a handsome bronze statue of the first president was placed atop the building. He has gazed serenely over his domain ever since.

JOHN MCMILLAN:
PASTOR AND EDUCATOR

The Scotch-Irish settlers who poured into western Pennsylvania following the Revolutionary War wasted no time in getting an educational system under way. In frontier days, the primary purpose of schools of higher education was to prepare students for the ministry. The clergy usually had more formal education than anybody else at that time, so it was natural that teaching school began to go hand in hand with ministerial duties. Schools were frequently set up in the manse itself, and students often boarded with the minister and his family. In fact, education sometimes became a church project, with ladies of the congregation working together to furnish clothing for the students. No fees were charged for board because most of the scholars could not afford to pay them.

Local historians debated for more than a century about which of three Washington County schools was the earliest. Was it that of the Reverend Joseph Smith at Buffalo, or the school established by Reverend Thaddeus Dod at Amity? Or perhaps it was the one begun by the Reverend John McMillan at Canonsburg. After a careful study of all the available evidence, most authorities agreed, finally, that Dr. McMillan's school was the first to be organized. But then the debate went on as to which of the three schools was the first to use a classical curriculum. Again, it has generally been agreed that the McMillan school was the first Latin school in the west, established during the winter of 1780–81. Dod's school began in 1782, and Smith's was organized in 1785. In any case, Dr. McMillan was such an unflagging champion of education during the early days of

Above, left: Pennsylvania State Historical Marker, located five miles north of Washington on Route 19. *Courtesy Mark Marietta, photographer.*

Above, right: Portrait of John McMillan. *Courtesy Bethel Presbyterian Church.*

Washington County that he earned the title of "the father of education in western Pennsylvania."

So, who was Dr. McMillan? John McMillan, also acknowledged as "the father of Presbyterianism in western Pennsylvania," was a towering figure in theological and educational affairs during the early days of Washington County. His Scotch-Irish parents had emigrated from County Antrim in Ireland to Chester County, Pennsylvania, where John McMillan was born in 1752. He attended school in Chester County and entered the College of New Jersey at Princeton, from which he was graduated in 1772.

Following graduation, McMillan studied theology with the Reverend Robert Smith, principal of the Pequea Academy, and was licensed to preach by the Presbytery of New Castle in October 1774. Ordained in June 1776, he embarked on a long and distinguished career, which was to take him to western Pennsylvania for a lifetime of teaching and ministering to the frontier settlements. He, his wife and baby arrived in Chartiers in the fall of 1778.

No sooner had McMillan accepted his post as pastor of the Chartiers Presbyterian Church than he opened his own log school. Within a decade,

McMillan, Smith and Dod were instrumental in organizing the Washington Academy, which was chartered in 1787. The trustees had difficulty in obtaining a principal for the new school but finally persuaded Dod to accept the post for one year. Classes began on April 1, 1789, in the Washington County courthouse, with twenty to thirty students attending. Dod was shortly succeeded as principal by David Johnston, a teacher of English at the academy.

Disaster struck within the next year, when the courthouse burned and the school had to suspend operations. Eager to get the academy back on its feet, McMillan and other trustees tried to persuade John Hoge to donate land for a building in Washington. Hoge refused, and efforts to arouse interest in the townspeople failed. The trustees then turned to Colonel John Canon, of Canonsburg, who not only gave a plot of ground but also advanced funds for the construction of a building. Thus it was that the Canonsburg Academy was founded in July 1791. McMillan had hoped to build the academy near his original log school, but after Colonel Canon offered both land and building funds, he stifled his disappointment and plunged wholeheartedly into the efforts to establish the new school.

Meantime, back in Washington, John Hoge changed his mind and decided to donate to Washington Academy a piece of land that is part of the present W&J campus. Impressed and somewhat shaken by the evident

Original log academy, erected by McMillan about 1780. Now restored, it sits today on the site of the former Jefferson College, Canonsburg. *From* History of Washington County, Vol. I.

enthusiasm for the Canonsburg Academy, the citizens of Washington were aroused and donated sufficient funds by 1793 to construct a new building for the Washington Academy. The legislature helped out by appropriating $3,000 for the project in 1796.

McMillan, who had continued to serve as a trustee of the Washington Academy, resigned in 1795 in order to devote his energies entirely to the Canonsburg Academy. He referred to the Canonsburg Academy as the "original fountain of science and literature in these western counties," suggesting that it was the continuation of his own school founded in 1780–81. In 1794, the legislature granted Canonsburg Academy a charter under the name of the Academy and Library Company of Canonsburg. In 1798, McMillan was elected honorary president. Almost immediately, a movement was begun to convert the academy into a college, and in 1802, Jefferson College was chartered with McMillan as president of the board of trustees. Since he could not serve both as a board member and a member of the faculty, McMillan resigned in order to become professor of divinity.

Four years later, in the spring of 1806, by act of the legislature, Washington Academy became Washington College. The unfortunate and sometimes bitter rivalry between the two schools, which had begun in the nineties, continued off and on for sixty years, until they finally joined to become Washington and Jefferson College in 1865. The united college owed much to John McMillan, who worked tirelessly to launch both schools; the continuing friction between them was no doubt a source of real dismay to him. However, he continued to work diligently on behalf of Jefferson College and never ceased in his efforts to improve education in western Pennsylvania.

McMillan remained as pastor at Chartiers Church until April 1830. He never really retired, for he continued to travel and preach extensively. In the fall of 1833, he fell ill after returning from a trip to Pittsburgh and died on Saturday, November 16, at the age of eighty-two. He was buried beside his wife in the cemetery of Chartiers Church.

Whiskey Rebellion: The Taxpayers' Revolt

No account of important events in eighteenth-century Washington County would be complete without at least a brief reference to the Whiskey Rebellion. This period of confusion, civil disorder and occasional terrorism dragged on for three miserable years, from July 1791 to November 1794. It must have been as unsettling to the ordinary citizen as the Indian menace. Life on the western Pennsylvania frontier during the 1790s was anything but dull.

Taxation, with or without representation, has been a trying burden for mankind since the dawn of organized government. So it was not surprising that the lusty and independent farmers in western Pennsylvania resented an excise tax on whiskey that had been levied by the federal government in March 1791. The law was passed in spite of determined opposition from the representatives of the western counties and particularly affected Allegheny, Westmoreland, Washington and Fayette. Farmers had thought they were finally rid of the pesky tax on spirits, for Pennsylvania had passed and repealed a succession of such taxes, mostly because attempts to collect them were futile. As far back as 1684, the Pennsylvania Assembly had tried to tax whiskey; other laws had been passed in 1738, 1744, 1756 and 1772. All had been eventually repealed.

The rebellious farmers had several reasons to despise the tax. Liquor was a useful fringe benefit provided for hired hands; people in the western provinces couldn't import it because of the distances involved, and besides, they were an independent lot and preferred to make their own brew anyway. In 1791, there were 272 licensed stills in Washington County, or roughly one for every twenty or thirty families. Roads through the mountains were poor; grain could be transported much more easily in liquid form. For instance, a packhorse could carry four bushels of rye; that same packhorse could carry the equivalent of twenty-four bushels of rye distilled into whiskey. There was less currency in circulation in the sparsely populated western regions. By 1792, the tax on a gallon of whiskey was seven cents; in the unsettled west, this amounted to about one quarter of the sales price. However, in the comfortable and settled east, it amounted to only about one eighth of the sales price. Thus the tax hit the hardest in the region where less money was available.

Another irritation was the provision that the stills, as well as the product, were to be taxed. This was too much. And the last straw was the requirement that any violators would be tried in federal courts. In those days, there were no federal courts west of the mountains.

Citizens who were so ill advised as to accept appointments as tax collectors were harassed mercilessly. One fellow named William Graham was accosted in his hotel room in the middle of the night by a disguised person who announced that he was Beelzebub and had come to fetch Graham and deliver him to other devils outside. Graham fled. Another collector named Robert Johnson was attacked by a gang of toughs who cut off his hair, took away his horse and left him tarred and feathered. He, too, departed in haste and resigned his commission.

The most outspoken protesters against the latest tax lost no time in getting organized. Committees for each of the four counties involved were formed to plan the resistance. A four-county committee met in September 1791 and denounced the excise law as unjust, oppressive and tending to bring misery and ruin to the western country. Several committees were appointed to present the case to Congress and to set up committees of correspondence. The protestors resolved that they would have no business dealings with any person who might accept the job as tax collector; they would "withhold comforts" and treat such persons with contempt, and they urged all citizens to do the same. It began to sound like 1776 all over again.

Led by David Bradford, John Holcroft and others, angry farmers committed numerous acts of vandalism and violence. Barns and mills were burned, and notes were left, signed "Tom the Tinker." The mysterious Tom, whose identity remained a secret until after the rebellion (it was alleged to be Holcroft), was given to writing threatening letters to persons suspected of paying the tax or even to those who did not vigorously oppose it.

The letters were placed in the houses of the suspects or nailed to nearby trees, and if the recipients did not publish them in a Pittsburgh newspaper and attend a meeting of the "whiskey boys," they could expect a visit from Tom and company. Stills were "tinkered with"—that is, they were shot full of holes. Throughout this period, entire families were threatened, terrified and abused. Sheriffs refused to serve warrants, and magistrates wailed that laws could not be enforced owing to the large numbers of people who opposed the taxes.

Events reached a fever pitch, and a virtual reign of terror existed during the summer of 1794. The house and other properties of prominent Allegheny County tax collector General John Neville were burned to the ground by a party of rebels. Shots were exchanged during this encounter, and one of the insurgent leaders, Major James McFarlane, was killed. This infuriated the whiskey boys, who, led by the fiery Bradford, organized a muster of some five thousand men at Braddock's field on August 1. The plan was to attack Pittsburgh. However, when the mob reached the city, it was wined and dined so hospitably by the citizenry that the attack never came off.

The Whiskey Boys depicts the fiery Bradford inciting revolt with the aim of capturing Pittsburgh. *Courtesy Ray W. Forquer, artist, and Countryside Prints, Inc.*

In the meantime, President Washington, after receiving numerous official reports about the uproar, had issued a proclamation summoning the militia to restore law and order to the unhappy region. Various groups of commissioners, appointed by the president and the governor of Pennsylvania, were already working frantically to formulate some plan to unseat the radical minority that was enforcing a rule of terror. The gravity of the whole affair was finally penetrating the consciousness of most of the rebel leaders, who, in one of their wildest moments, had even helped Bradford raid the United States mail. The prospect of facing an army of thirteen thousand men, composed of troops from Virginia, Maryland and New Jersey as well as Pennsylvania, was very sobering. The army was under the command of Major General Henry (Light Horse Harry) Lee. Lee was the father of Robert E. Lee, who was to lead a rebellion himself some seventy years later.

The troops came, resistance melted and, when the dust had settled, Bradford had skipped out to Louisiana, then under the control of Spain, where he spent the rest of his life at Bayou Sara as a wealthy planter. Twenty prisoners were marched off to Philadelphia for trial; two were convicted, and two were pardoned by the president. In August 1795, general and special pardons were granted by the president and the governor to those who had not been indicted or had been vindicated of crimes related to the insurrection. Bradford himself was pardoned by President John Adams on March 9, 1799. In addition to the individual personal and financial losses, this three-year caper cost the United States government $669,992.34.

David Bradford: Rebel with a Cause

Since the Bradford House Historical Association reenacts the escape of David Bradford in the fall of each year, it is interesting to go back to the tempestuous days of the 1790s and look at the fiery and talented young man who created such a sensation during the Whiskey Rebellion. He was only about thirty-four years old when he fled.

The story of David Bradford is one of the most intriguing and romantic adventures to take place in western Pennsylvania. Bradford, an ambitious, brilliant young lawyer, came to Washington in 1782 from his native Maryland, where he was born about 1760. Court records show that in April 1782 he was the sixth attorney to be admitted to practice law in the Washington County Courts. Within a short time, he had established a successful practice; by 1783, he had been appointed deputy attorney general for Washington County. By 1788, he had become affluent enough to build the first stone house in town on South Main Street. By frontier standards, it probably ranked as a mansion. The handsome stairway was solid mahogany; the mantelpieces and other interior furnishings were imported from Philadelphia and had to be transported across the Alleghenies at considerable expense.

The able newcomer had important family connections when he came to town. Two of his sisters were already settled in the community. Agnes Bradford had married John McDowell, who was very prominent in legal circles. It was McDowell who had helped his new neighbor, John McMillan, when the pastor and his family first arrived at Chartiers. McDowell had purchased a four-hundred-acre tract of land near Chartiers Creek; on this

This mahogany staircase was said to have been imported from England at a guinea a step. The Bradford House, by frontier standards, was a palace. *From* History of Washington County, Vol. 1.

property, he had constructed the log cabin in which McMillan had preached his first sermon in Washington County. McDowell was also one of the first elders of the Chartiers Church and one of the first three commissioners of Washington County upon its formation in 1781. He served in numerous legislative and judicial capacities until his death in 1809 at the age of seventy-three.

Jane Bradford, another sister, married Colonel James Allison, who had settled in the Chartiers Valley in 1774. Allison bought one thousand acres in the region and settled on a tract known as Mount Pleasant. He, too, was an elder in McMillan's Chartiers Church. An able lawyer, he served with his brother-in-law, Judge McDowell, as an associate judge of Washington County and as one of the first trustees of Washington Academy. Both McDowell and Allison were also among the first trustees of the Canonsburg Academy.

Against this family background of excellence in civic and judicial leadership, the brash young brother-in-law of the two judges began to assume an influential role in educational and political—as well as legal—circles. He joined McDowell and Allison as members of the board of trustees for Washington Academy and was appointed to the all-important building committee. The committee had work to do, since the school's first quarters had been destroyed in the courthouse fire of 1791. In July 1793, the members were charged by the board as follows: "A house should be built out of the moneys subscribed—thirty by thirty-five feet, of stone or brick, or as the committee should direct."

Even though a building program for the academy was obviously a matter of some urgency for the homeless school, many of the board members had even more pressing matters on their minds. They were thoroughly distracted by the escalating protest over the tax on whiskey that had been levied by the federal government in 1791. It will be remembered that the farmers in western Pennsylvania were particularly upset by the excise, and a four-county committee, composed of representatives of Fayette, Washington, Allegheny and Westmoreland, had been spearheading an organized protest for the past two years.

Events were roaring to a climax during the summer of 1794, and the impetuous Bradford was in the thick of the fight: in fact, he was leading it. While many of his friends and neighbors were sympathetic to the cause, they were not eager to protest as vigorously as Bradford and the militant farmers. And John McMillan was so adamant that the law must be upheld that he once refused to administer communion to his flock unless they indicated a willingness (however reluctant) to obey the law.

Unfortunately for his promising career in western Pennsylvania, Bradford became so converted to the cause of insurrection that he eventually became the most prominent and powerful leader in the resistance against the government. His defiance led him to plan a robbery of the United States mail; the pouch was delivered to the Black Horse Tavern in Canonsburg and examined there by Bradford, John Canon and several others. They were looking for information concerning the attitudes of various people in the region about the progress of the resistance. A few critical letters from some prominent citizens in Pittsburgh so enraged the group that they decided on an audacious plan to call out the militia to plunder and destroy the city. Bradford's mob of about five thousand met on August 1, 1794, at Braddock's field near Pittsburgh and marched on the city; however, they were so diverted by large quantities of whiskey supplied by the nervous citizens that they soon lost all interest in fighting, and the "attack" never really came off.

When the news of the alarming events in western Pennsylvania reached President Washington, he concluded that it was time to summon the militia to enforce the law and to restore order to the unhappy region. By this time, some of Bradford's followers realized with dismay that they were flirting with treason. Some of those who were marking time camped on the grounds of Washington Academy were puzzled by the president's action. "Call out the militia against us?" they wondered. "We *are* the militia. Then we will be fighting ourselves!"

The militia, fifteen thousand strong from Virginia, Maryland, New Jersey and Pennsylvania, did come, and in October 1794, special orders were issued for Bradford's arrest. The still popular leader had friends who kept him posted about military movements, and on October 25,

The Old Black Horse Tavern, Canonsburg, Pennsylvania, was a vital seat of the Whiskey Insurrection in 1794. Presumably, Bradford rifled mail sacks containing General Neville's reports with evidence against the insurrectionists. J. Howard Iams, artist. *Courtesy Westmoreland Museum of American Art.*

he was warned of the approach of a cavalry unit intent on his capture. Located in his handsome Washington home, he hastily departed through a rear window and galloped off into the night on the spirited gray horse that had served him so well during the summer campaign. With soldiers in hot pursuit (there was a price of $500 on his head), Bradford made it to McKees Rocks that night. There he traded his faithful horse for a skiff and set out down the Ohio River. A touch-and-go gun battle with his pursuers went on all night, but he managed to slip through by staying close to the opposite shore of the river.

The next night, Bradford encountered the skipper of a keelboat who was also fleeing the region for his own part in the rebellion. Just as they were about to depart for New Orleans the next morning, a party of soldiers boarded the boat. The crew of the keelboat helped to disarm the troops and throw them in the river, pelting them all the while with lumps of the coal

Above: *Bradford's Escape.* This 1920s mural by artist Malcolm Parcell is in the George Washington Hotel, Washington, Pennsylvania. *Courtesy Washington County Historical Society.*

Below: The house, built by David Bradford in 1788, where Rebecca Harding Davis was born. *Courtesy Ray W. Forquer, artist, and Countryside Prints, Inc.*

cargo aboard the boat. The soggy soldiers sloshed ashore while the keelboat headed down the river.

Bradford finally made it to Louisiana, which then belonged to Spain. He settled down at Bayou Sara, where his wife eventually joined him, and became a wealthy planter. Legend has it that after his pardon by President John Adams in March 1799, he returned to Washington at least once, probably about 1801, to take care of some business matters.

In 1959, the Pennsylvania Historical and Museum Commission assumed control of the Bradford House. It had changed hands many times during the 170 years since its construction and had been altered considerably. The commission restored the building to the "architectural showpiece of the eighteenth century" that it once was; it is now the oldest building in Washington and one of the most historic sites in the county.

Founding of the *Reporter*

It was on August 15, 1808, that William Sample and William B. Brown printed the first issue of the *Reporter* in a tavern named the Sign of the Swan where they had set up shop. The two men came to Washington in a wagon that hauled their printing press, type and other equipment. The editors had first considered establishing their paper in Waynesburg, but events "which concern ourselves alone, combined with circumstances of a political nature, have determined us to establish it here."

When Sample and Brown came to town to publish their four-page weekly, they found a busy little community of about one thousand people. Most of the houses were built of brick or logs. There was only one stone building, and a few structures were covered with weatherboarding. There were numerous inns and taverns to take care of the steady stream of pioneers headed west. Washington was fortunately situated on a through road to the frontier and became even busier with the tourist trade as the years went by and the National Road was completed. In addition to the Sign of the Swan, other establishments sported some very exotic names, such as the Sign of the Indian Queen, the Sign of the Black Bear, the Spread Eagle, the Mermaid and, of course, the famous Globe Inn. Main Street, then known as Market Street, was lined with log buildings. The courthouse was a small, square brick building with an adjoining jail. Up on the hill was Washington College, which had been in operation for several years; the handsome administration building, built in 1793, dominated the hill.

During the early days, the *Reporter* printed very little local news. People wanted to know what was going on in the outside world, and besides, they knew the local news long before it could get into print. Reports trickled in so slowly in those days before the telegraph that "news" was sometimes history before it was published in the paper. The major news story that preoccupied the *Reporter* for its first two months of life was a red-hot race for governor of Pennsylvania. The election of 1808 was just two months off, and the campaign was in full swing. The candidates were James Ross, a Federalist, and Simon Snyder, a Democratic-Republican. The *Reporter* supported Snyder and all other candidates of the Democratic-Republican party, including James Madison for president of the United States and George Clinton for vice president.

James Ross, one of western Pennsylvania's earliest and most prominent lawyers, was born in York County in 1762. He taught for a time at McMillan's Academy in Canonsburg and was admitted to the Washington County bar in 1795. Ross was first elected to political office in 1794 as U.S. senator from Pennsylvania. A strong Federalist, he was defeated in his bid for governor in 1799 and 1802. In 1808, he decided to try again. The editors accused Ross of supporting perpetual and odious taxes on retailers' licenses, carriages, stamps, auctions and domestic sugar. It was pointed out in the paper right up to Election Day on October 11, 1808, that the public life and conduct of Ross was such that "it would be dangerous to elect such a man." Voters were told to "beware of the Federalists and their candidate, James Ross; he is the most violent of Federalists. Make him your Governor, and depend upon it, it will not be his fault if you are not eased of the trouble of electing another." He supported the sedition laws and wanted a standing army and navy; he was alleged to be the enemy of peace and of the Irish, German and other immigrants.

The campaign took a rather nasty turn as even the religious qualifications of Ross were attacked; he was accused of being an enemy of Christianity. The *Reporter* noted that the Federalists boasted of the religion of their candidate and wondered how Ross could be pushed as a religious man. It was reported that Ross had stated it was not a necessary qualification for public office that a person should "acknowledge the being of God and a future state of rewards and punishments."

At this point, the Reverend John McMillan, DD, the "Presbyterian Pope," entered the fray in support of Ross. The editors of the *Reporter* could not conceal their astonishment at the following letter, which they printed in their editorial column, with numerous lamentations:

This is to certify that I have been intimately acquainted with James Ross, Esq., of Pittsburgh, for more than 30 years; that I never heard him speak, or heard of him speaking disrespectfully of religion or religious persons…I know nothing, nor have I ever heard anything against his moral character that could in the smallest disqualify him for the office of Governor…I am determined to give him all the support in my power, and hope that all the friends of religion and good order will do the same.

John McMillan Washington Co., Aug. 29, 1808.

The editors quoted, "Thou shalt not bear false witness" and wondered how McMillan could reconcile his strict obedience to this commandment and yet make such a statement. They hoped that "for the honor of human nature," the declaration was true, but there were too many circumstances to the contrary to convince them to believe it. They concluded that "between Mr. McMillan and his God be its truth or falsehood determined."

Simon Snyder, the Democratic-Republican candidate, was the son of a German immigrant who spent his early years working as a tanner, storekeeper and farmer. He was elected to the legislature and became Speaker of the House. Snyder disliked pomp and ceremony and was portrayed during the campaign as a friend of the people and of equal rights. Editors of the *Reporter* liked him because he was a friend of peace, a believer in God, a lover of Republican simplicity and a man of mild and amiable disposition.

On October 10, the editors urged all voters to exercise "one of the noblest privileges of man, that of electing your rulers." They were, of course, expected to vote for Simon Snyder. On Monday, October 17, the paper joyously reported a "Triumph of Principle" because the election on the previous Tuesday had resulted in victory for Snyder and defeat for Ross and presumably for Federalism as well.

More than two hundred years have rolled by since the *Reporter* fought its first political campaign, and these years have brought many changes to the paper. First of all, it has survived, while other local journals, published for varying periods of time since 1795, eventually perished. The *Reporter* itself changed hands many times. Brown sold his interest to Sample in 1810, and Sample was the sole proprietor until 1833. Between 1833 and 1873, the paper was bought and sold about a dozen times. In 1873, E.L. Christman took charge for the second time (he had a brief association with the paper in the 1850s), and three generations of the Christman family were connected with the paper for the next sixty years. On August 4, 1876, it became a daily paper.

The Strean Building was erected in 1860 on South Main Street in Washington and housed the offices of the *Reporter* on its upper floors for many years. The newspaper later moved to Brownson Avenue before moving to its current location on South Main Street in 1923. The *Reporter* was purchased in 1903 by Observer Publishing Co. Founded in 1808, today's *Observer-Reporter* is one of the nation's oldest continuously operating daily newspapers. *Courtesy* Washington Observer-Reporter.

In 1903, the *Reporter* was purchased by the Observer Publishing Company and printed as the company's afternoon newspaper, while the *Observer* was published by the same company as a morning paper. In May 1967, the two papers were united under the same masthead, the *Observer-Reporter*. The morning edition carries Greene County as well as Washington County news, while the evening edition is primarily of interest to Washington County readers.

The *Observer-Reporter* today continues to hold its place on the honor roll of the oldest daily newspapers in the nation—those that were established during the period from 1764 to 1808.

War Between the Colleges

The disastrous fire during the winter of 1790–91 that deprived Washington County of its first courthouse also left the fledgling Washington Academy homeless. Plans to proceed with the construction of a new courthouse began almost immediately. However, the future for Washington Academy was not so rosy. In vain did the prestigious John McMillan, Thaddeus Dod and David Johnston, principal of the academy, plead with the townspeople for financial help to get the school back on its feet. It was a futile effort. Years later, in 1817, McMillan wrote of the attempt to rebuild the school in Washington. He reported, with more than a suggestion of disgust, that "so indifferent were the inhabitants of that town to the interests of literature in general and to the demand of the church in particular that notwithstanding the state's donation an academy could not be supported."

What to do? The trustees took their problem to Colonel John Canon, eight miles away. It so happened that Canon and other McMillan supporters had hoped for some time to found an academy in Canonsburg, either by enlarging the McMillan school or starting a new one. Here was their chance. In almost no time at all, a group of men, including Canon and McMillan, found themselves meeting after church one day in a field "under the shade of some sassafras bushes." Exercises were held that July day in 1791 invoking the blessing of God upon a new academic institution. It began that very fall, holding classes in temporary quarters until Colonel Canon's fine new stone building, being constructed on land he had donated, was ready. Canonsburg Academy was in business. It continued the work begun by McMillan in his own log school in 1780–81 that was alleged to be the "first literary institution west of the mountains." In 1792, the *Pittsburgh Gazette* advertised that the building for Canonsburg Academy was finished and that the grammar school was in operation under the direction of David Johnston, the former principal of the Washington Academy. Course offerings included English, geometry, trigonometry, astronomy, algebra and bookkeeping. Board was available in the neighborhood. The institution had the financial support of the Redstone Presbytery.

In 1794, the school was chartered by the Pennsylvania legislature as the Academy and Library Company of Canonsburg, with the continued enthusiastic moral and financial support of Presbyterians throughout the region. Contributions flowed in to repay Colonel Canon for the funds he had advanced for the building and to pay faculty salaries and help young men who were studying for the ministry.

By 1800, a movement was underway to convert the academy into a college, and McMillan, along with three others, drafted a petition for presentation to the legislature. Their efforts were successful, and Canonsburg Academy officially became Jefferson College on January 15, 1802. Its first president was John Watson, a son-in-law of John McMillan. By 1816, the college had outgrown Colonel Canon's original stone building. A new structure, College Hall, was built in 1816–17 on Central Avenue property bought from Canon's widow. In 1833, a third building, Providence Hall, was constructed at the same location.

In the meantime, back in Washington, the leading citizens now regretted their decision to rebuff McMillan and his friends. John Hoge finally donated land, and, through the joint efforts of the townspeople and the Pennsylvania legislature, a second building for Washington Academy was begun in 1793. In 1806, Washington College also received a charter from the Pennsylvania legislature. The stage was then set for an intercollegiate rivalry that continued for more than half a century. The circumstances that destroyed the quarters of the Washington Academy and resulted in the founding of the Canonsburg Academy created an ideal situation for the "college war," which continued off and on for years. The two institutions drew students from the same area, and this fact alone began to place a strain on the financial resources of both. Another complicating issue was the fact that the two schools even shared two presidents, Andrew Wylie and Matthew Brown.

As early as September 1815, there were serious suggestions to unite the two schools, and committees at both institutions were appointed to

Jefferson College, ca. 1850. Courtesy Ray W. Forquer, artist, and Countryside Prints, Inc.

explore this possibility. Jefferson students wanted the school to be situated in Canonsburg. Washington folk wanted their college to remain where it was. The fat was really in the fire when, in 1817, Andrew Wylie, DD and president of Jefferson College, was lured to that same post at Washington College. Jefferson trustees were outraged at Wylie's defection and refused to discuss the matter of unity any further. Accusations and communications, both public and private, flew briskly between the two campuses until 1820. Even the Presbyterian Synod tried, without success, to unite the two schools at Washington. Nothing more was done about unification until the 1860s.

As if things weren't already complicated enough, there was the matter of Matthew Brown's appointment to the presidency of Jefferson College in 1822. This development resulted from a bitter feud in Washington about the desirability of the same man holding both the presidency of Washington College and the pastorate of the First Presbyterian Church. The occupant of both hot seats was the Reverend Dr. Brown, who had been serving as Washington College's first president since 1806. Caught between two

Washington College, ca. 1840. Courtesy Ray W. Forquer, artist, and Countryside Prints, Inc.

opposing political factions, he resigned as president of Washington College in 1817.

This was the point at which Wylie, late of Jefferson College, took over. Brown remained in Washington as pastor of the First Presbyterian Church for five years. In 1822, depressed by the death of his wife and the complicated state of affairs between the college and his church, Brown decided to quit Washington entirely and head west. Before leaving, he called on his good friend Samuel Ralston, who happened to be president of Jefferson College's board of trustees. The board was looking for a new president and offered the job to Brown. He decided to take it, and his acceptance resulted in a twenty-three-year period of greatness for Jefferson College. During his administration, 772 students graduated, three times as many as under his predecessors. A strong and decisive leader, he was more compatible with the Canonsburg community than with Washington. Prior to his appearance on campus, Jefferson College had just survived a period of student rebellion, and the trustees were relieved to obtain a man of strength to run things.

After Brown's tenure drew to a close in 1845, Jefferson continued for another twenty years under four presidents, whose terms ranged from two to eleven years. Financial problems were an ever-present worry—the college had always been poor. It had no endowment for the first fifty years of its existence. Finally, it raised $60,000 by selling "cheap scholarships." This was no help, for it then lost income from student fees, since every student secured a scholarship that entitled him to free tuition. During its sixty-three years of existence, the student body only once approached 300, yet it graduated 1,950 men. Of these, 940 went into the ministry, 428 became lawyers and 208 were physicians. A large number served as college presidents, governors and army officers. Two became members of presidential cabinets, sixty were in the Congress, sixty on the bench and eighteen achieved high ecclesiastical office.

The Civil War proved to be the undoing of Jefferson College. The school's financial resources were not equal to the demands as costs increased at the end of the war. The conflict itself depleted the ranks of the student body as men departed to enlist with both Union and Confederacy. Two hundred

"Old Main, 1905." The heart of the campus, Old Main was constructed in the early 1830s. The two towers were added in 1865 to symbolize the joining of the two colleges, Washington and Jefferson. *Photogravure from* The Art of Washington County.

forty-six alumni served in one army or the other; thirty-six died in service with the U.S. Army, while eleven gave their lives for the Confederacy. Back in Canonsburg, the situation became so desperate that, in 1865, by action of the boards of trustees of both schools, Washington and Jefferson Colleges were at last united.

The Road to Prosperity

During the first decade of the nineteenth century, Washington County was primarily an agricultural region with a population of about thirty-five thousand. Since 1790, it had been the largest county west of the Alleghenies and was destined to hold this lead until 1830. For nearly a century after its settlement, the county remained largely agricultural. The oil and gas industries were not developed until the 1880s (although gas was discovered in the area as early as 1821). Similarly, the presence of coal had been noted as far back as 1771 by George Washington during a visit to western Pennsylvania with his friend, Colonel William Crawford. But the development of the coalfields also lay several decades in the future. The growth of Washington County as a manufacturing and industrial area, as well as an agricultural one, began with the National Road.

Until the completion of the National Pike from Washington, Pennsylvania, to Wheeling, West Virginia, in 1818, this rural region was served by the most primitive methods of transportation. The first settlers to cross the Alleghenies pushed their way through on Indian trails and military "roads" dating from French and Indian War days. These old routes were so rudimentary that even wagons could not be accommodated. This was the period of the packhorse—a poor, lowly animal, whose role, according to historian Earle Forrest, has been sadly underrated in the settlement of the frontier. These sturdy animals carried on their backs family furniture, lumber, merchandise of all kinds, stoves and even babies—for the infants rode while their elders traveled by foot alongside.

The "S" Bridge on the National Road. Courtesy Ray W. Forquer, artist, and Countryside Prints, Inc.

In time, as wider roads were cut through the wilderness from Braddock's Road into Washington County, the packhorse gradually gave way to the Conestoga wagon. Even wider roads did not always help, however, for they were likely to be axle deep in mud for months at a time. Thus many merchants continued to use the reliable packhorse until the National Road was completed through Washington County. This road so revolutionized transportation and travel in this area that it brought an economic boom to Washington and Washington County that lasted until the middle of the nineteenth century.

The National Road was the first highway authorized and paid for by the federal government. On March 29, 1806, President Jefferson signed into law the National Road Act that had been approved by the Ninth Congress in late 1805. This act finally set into motion the building of a road whose construction had first concerned George Washington shortly after the Revolutionary War. It was to explore the possibility of a great road across the Alleghenies, connecting the east with the Ohio Valley, that George Washington made a trip in 1784 from the Potomac to the Ohio River.

On this journey, he met for the first time Albert Gallatin, a gifted man whose career as statesman and diplomat was just beginning. Gallatin, too, had been interested in the construction of such a road, and the route he proposed to Washington at their first meeting in a hunter's cabin near the Monongahela River was the one that Washington agreed would be most suitable. It was Gallatin who, as secretary of the treasury under Jefferson and Madison, was one of the principal promoters of this first national highway. While Washington continued to push for construction of the road during his years as president, nothing came of it during his administration or that of John Adams. After the admission of Ohio as a state in 1803, agitation for the road increased; among its strongest and most influential supporters were Henry Clay, John C. Calhoun and T.M.T. McKennan of Washington.

In 1811, funds were appropriated and work was finally begun at Cumberland, Maryland. Construction was costly and tedious. From Cumberland, the road continued to Frostburg and Grantsville, Maryland, and crossed obliquely through southwestern Pennsylvania for some eighty miles from Uniontown to West Alexander. It entered Washington County over the Monongahela River at West Brownsville. Several Washington County communities owe their origins to the pike, including Centerville (halfway between Uniontown and Washington), Beallsville and, of course, Claysville, which was named for Henry Clay, one of the road's greatest champions.

The right of way for the new road was sixty-six feet. The roadbed was thirty-two feet, twenty of which were laid with broken and impacted stones eighteen inches deep. The average cost of the entire road to Wheeling, its western terminus in 1818, was $13,000 per mile, a whopping sum of money in those days. Even before its completion, the road was successful beyond

Conestoga on the National Road. Part of a mural by Malcolm Parcell in the George Washington Hotel. *Courtesy Washington County Historical Society.*

The Arrival of Henry Clay. Clay, a strong supporter of the National Road, was a frequent visitor to Washington. He had many friends there, and his son attended Washington College. Part of a mural by Malcolm Parcell in the George Washington Hotel. *Courtesy Washington County Historical Society.*

Lafayette's Visit. Part of a mural by Malcolm Parcell in the George Washington Hotel commemorating the visit of Lafayette to Washington. *Courtesy of Washington County Historical Society.*

its wildest expectations. Almost overnight, it became the most important route for travelers, freight and mail between the east and the middle west. The federally funded road eventually reached Vandalia, Illinois, some eight hundred miles from Cumberland.

To Washington County, in particular, it spelled prosperity. The long lines of Conestogas and Concord coaches carried passengers, wagoners and drivers who needed the services of inns and taverns. This was the heyday of Malden Tavern, Century Inn, Charley Hill Tavern, Cross Keys, Mount Vernon House, LaFayette Inn and many others. Washington was transformed from a little frontier village to a bustling center of national importance. Carriage and wagon making became big businesses. Several local companies built hundreds of Conestoga wagons, farm wagons, carriages and stagecoaches. Milestone markers, made of iron, provided another industry for western Pennsylvania, as one foundry at Brownsville and another at Connellsville had the contract for delivering the markers between Cumberland and Wheeling. Tollhouses were built for the toll keepers who collected fees for animals, pedestrians and vehicles that traveled the road.

In fact, the road created such a brisk business for the Washington area that the proposed construction of a railroad through the county during the 1830s encountered bitter opposition from wagoners, stage drivers, blacksmiths, wagon makers and tavern keepers. They managed to convince the public

Toll House at West Alexander. Malcolm Parcell, artist. *Courtesy Dr. E. Ronald Salvitti.*

One of the last freight Conestogas in western Pennsylvania. In 1922, while visiting in Washington County, Henry Ford saw this wagon near Hickory and wanted it for his collection. D.C. Miller, the owner, presented it to him as a gift. *From* History of Washington County, Vol. 1.

that their jobs would be on the line if the railroad came through. Indeed, the most prosperous period for southwestern Pennsylvania was between 1844, when the railroad reached Cumberland, and 1852. Travelers to the west disembarked from trains at Cumberland and continued by coach over the National Road. The discovery of gold in California also increased traffic immensely. Sadly, all this came to a shrieking halt when, in May 1852, a Pennsylvania Railroad train chugged into Pittsburgh. The predictions of the wagoners and drivers came true almost overnight. Thousands were thrown out of work, taverns closed and weeds began to take over the roadway.

After the Civil War, the historic old road was used mostly for local travel. It was rescued from oblivion after the turn of the century by the automobile. As U.S. Route 40, it continues to carry traffic from coast to coast. In Pennsylvania, a few historic sites still exist to remind motorists of the glorious old days when picturesque and interesting characters traveled this first national highway. A restored tollhouse near Uniontown, a few milestone markers and several sturdy stone and brick bridges are still in existence.

WESTWARD HO!

L ucius W. Stockton comes down through the pages of history as one of those energetic, dashing, enterprising and capable characters who seem to belong mostly in fiction. Born in Flemington, New Jersey, in 1799 to a family that had long been prominent in colonial affairs (his great-uncle Richard Stockton was a New Jersey signer of the Declaration of Independence, and his grandfather was famed as the "Revolutionary Preacher"), Stockton got into the transportation business at an early age. For a quarter of a century, he was the best-known man along the National Road from Baltimore to Wheeling, and for the twenty-year period from 1824 to 1844, he was the leading stagecoach proprietor in the United States.

With the completion of the National Road from Cumberland to Wheeling in 1818, the beginning of an exciting and romantic period in the annals of American transportation was under way. For the next forty years, life for the people in the towns and villages on the road had a special adventurous quality. Stagecoaches and mail coaches raced along the nation's first federally financed highway in a neverending stream. It was not unusual for twenty-four horse-drawn vehicles to be lined up in a seemingly endless procession at the same time. The slower Conestogas rumbled steadily at a more plodding pace, laden with settlers and possessions headed west. Long caravans of animals—horses, mules, cattle, hogs and sheep—wound their way down the length of the road, all of them part of one of the greatest peaceful migrations in history. It was a giant kaleidoscope of human and animal life on the move.

There were, of course, many stage operators during the heyday of the road—Stockton's company was by no means the only one—but it was one of the most interesting because of the colorful character who owned the business. In 1821, Stockton and his partner, Richard Stokes, began operation of a small passenger line from Gettysburg to Hagerstown. This provided a connecting link for travelers between the National Road and the eastern turnpikes. An advertisement in the *Reporter* that year offered passengers weekly service east via Gettysburg and Hagerstown until April 1. After that date, runs were made three times weekly. The line promised to transport passengers safely and speedily from Wheeling and Pittsburgh to Philadelphia and other eastern cities, a distance of more than 350 miles, in little more than four days!

When Stockton and Stokes extended their operations into western Pennsylvania and Little Washington, Daniel Moore was added to the partnership. The firm was named the National Road Stage Company. Eventually, it absorbed many smaller lines and soon offered through service from Wheeling to Baltimore and Washington, D.C.

And what an exciting trip it was, both for passengers and road watchers along the route! There was a dramatic quality about the sturdy mail and passenger coaches as they were drawn swiftly along the road by teams of magnificent, spirited horses. They kept a remarkably accurate time schedule, in spite of bad weather and heavy traffic, day and night. It was said that farmers could tell the time by the regular passage of the coaches on the road. They stopped every twelve miles or so to change horses—and sometimes drivers—at taverns placed conveniently on the route. Usually drivers of passenger coaches were responsible for one team. Mail drivers, however, might drive three or four teams that were changed and cared for by grooms along the way.

These regular stops gave passersby and road watchers an opportunity to witness all the excitement involved in switching the teams. They might even be lucky enough to see the likes of Henry Clay, John Quincy Adams, Daniel Webster, Andrew Jackson or other important statesmen of the day get out to stretch their legs. On one occasion, when a coach in which Clay was traveling overturned, he was reported to have got up, dusted himself off and remarked, "This is mixing the clay of Kentucky with the limestone of Pennsylvania." The rest stop over, the horses were hitched to the stage, and all hands climbed aboard once again. The equipage then took off in a great cloud of dust. Coaches traveled rather consistently at a breakneck speed. Usually, passengers all rode inside,

Hill's Tavern, Scenery Hill. Now the Century Inn, it is the oldest continually kept tavern on the National Road. *Courtesy Ray W. Forquer, artist.*

but occasionally, if things got crowded, one was allowed to ride on the coveted seat beside the driver.

Through the years, Stockton built his National Stage Company into a line second to none. He managed his operations carefully. Agents were on duty in every town between Wheeling and Baltimore, usually in a leading hostelry, which frequently bore the name National Hotel. In Little Washington, his agency was in a hotel by that name, in a building constructed by Moore on the northwest corner of South Main and Maiden Streets. The building was later known as the Auld House.

Stockton's personal relationship with Little Washington deepened when, in November 1824, he married Moore's daughter, Rebecca. The family settled in Uniontown, in a fine home named Ben Lomond. Stockton's daughter, Margaret, was dubbed "Princess of the Pike" because of her frequent trips along the road between Uniontown and Washington to visit her grandfather.

She had no trouble claiming the coveted seat beside the driver of the stage. Margaret grew up and married Dr. Thomas McKennan, a prominent Washington physician and son of Tommy McKennan, and moved to the McKennan home on Maiden Street, where she lived until her death in 1924 at the age of ninety-three.

In the meantime, Stockton continued his successful stage operations from his home in Uniontown. He opened a line between Little Washington and Pittsburgh and established a tri-weekly service between Washington and Cadiz, Ohio, where passengers could connect with Wooster, Cleveland and other Lake Erie points. Typical fare schedules for the period called for a fee of $10.00 from Pittsburgh to Baltimore and $13.00 from Pittsburgh to Philadelphia. Two dollars would buy a ticket from Baltimore to Frederick or from Frederick to Hagerstown and from Little Washington to Wheeling. From Uniontown to Little Washington, the fee was $2.25.

Stockton himself took off on inspection trips on a regular basis. He traveled from Uniontown to Cumberland in one day, stopping at way stations along the route to transact business. From Cumberland to Hagerstown, a distance of sixty-six miles, was also only a day's trip for the tireless Stockton, who by then had been nicknamed "the Flying Dutchman." The journey from Uniontown to Wheeling required a mere twelve hours. His two favorite sorrel mares, Bet and Sal, were treated to water laced with spirits at their rest stops, and it was said that the mares reached the point where they would drink only whiskey-flavored water.

Stories about Stockton were legion. One of the favorites was about the time he was alleged to have raced a B&O locomotive in the days before trains were taken seriously. The race began at a relay station just west of Baltimore, and according to legend, Stockton won handily. Another time, on a coach, his spirited team took off on the run. Stockton was accompanied on that occasion by his wife and sister. The latter became much alarmed and

The famous Stokes versus Stockton horse and steam race. The horse actually won! *From* Railroads in the Days of Steam.

The last stage to leave Washington on completion of the railroad between Washington and Pittsburgh, May 18, 1871. This was the first round-bodied coach constructed west of the mountains. Afterward, it was taken west and run on the plains. *From* History of Washington County, Vol 1.

a trifle hysterical, but Stockton, a master of the reins himself, soon had the runaways under control.

One of Stockton's strongest competitors was the Good Intent Line, operated by the partnership of Shriver, Steele and Company. The rivalry between the two companies was one of the hottest in the business. One of the Good Intent's drivers, Pete Burdine, came up with the following bit of doggerel: "If you take a seat in Stockton's line, you are sure to be passed by Pete Burdine."

So it was a boisterous, lusty, competitive business, and for one who loved it as much as Lucius Stockton, it was a shame that it came to an end so abruptly. He died in 1844, at the age of only forty-five, of blood poisoning contracted as the result of a dog bite. But then he was spared the distress of standing by as his beloved horses and coaches faded into history in their doomed contest with the iron horse.

KING COAL

In order to understand the beginnings of the coal industry in Washington County, we might do well to go back more than two hundred million years and find out how it all started. Millions of years ago, the region we know as Pennsylvania was covered by the sea. At intervals over many thousands of years, the land alternately rose above the sea and was submerged by it.

During those periods when the land was above sea level, trees, ferns and other forms of plant life grew in abundance. When the sea rushed in again, the vegetation was submerged under tons of sand and water. As this cycle was repeated over and over, the alternating layers of sand and rotting vegetation created substances that were to be very useful to Pennsylvanians in the centuries ahead.

Thus the natural resources we know today as coal, sandstone, shale and limestone came into being and lay waiting for the enterprising eighteen-, nineteenth- and twentieth-century inhabitants of the region to put them to good use. Washington County lies within the heart of one of the richest coal regions in the world—the great Appalachian coalfield. An area known as the "Pittsburgh seam" includes some eight thousand square miles of southwestern Pennsylvania. The bituminous coal found here is particularly valuable in manufacturing coke and gas; various grades are also used for fuel, home heating and numerous other purposes.

The rich coal deposits in western Pennsylvania were known to settlers as early as the 1760s. Colonel William Crawford called it to the attention of his good friend George Washington during one of the general's visits to the area about 1771. Coal formations uncovered through the centuries by erosion were also plainly visible on hillsides and along the banks of streams throughout southwestern Pennsylvania, as well as in Washington County. As roads were hacked out of the wilderness, seams of coal began to appear as the soft layer of topsoil was gradually worn away.

The first coal bank in the county to receive any attention was one located within the limits of Bassett Town in 1781, near where College Field is today. A few years later, when Colonel John Canon laid out his town in 1788, one of the bonuses provided for purchasers of his land was free coal from his bank "forever." By 1800, Dr. Absalom Baird owned a coal bank that became something of a little "community mine" for a number of years. In 1802, Judge James Allison began mining operations in his coal bank near McGovern. It was chiefly used for blacksmithing. Sometimes hauled for a considerable distance, the coal was sold for twenty-five cents per bushel.

It was between 1820 and 1830 that commercial coal mining on a small scale began in Washington County. These early operations used methods that were downright quaint when compared to today's sophisticated mining

This interior photo of an early twentieth-century coal mine illustrates the dark and dangerous work. *Courtesy Washington County Historical Society.*

techniques. In fact, they were done mostly by hand. In those days, it was a seasonal business: the first fields to be worked were near the Monongahela River, which provided the means of transporting the coal to market during the spring and summer months. Several one- to three-acre lots near Limetown were owned by John Jenkins, Enoch Cox, Samuel French and Jesse Bentley. Coal was hauled out of the pits by hand and piled on the riverbank, where it awaited shipment in the spring. As these early pits were worked, miners would burrow into a hillside horizontally and remove the coal in wheelbarrows. Eventually, rooms were formed on either side of the opening, and pillars were carved to support the roof. Large chunks of coal were broken into pieces for transportation to the riverbank. A laborer was supposed to be able to dig up to one hundred bushels of coal a day. At the riverbank in the spring or summer, the coal was loaded aboard boats called French Creeks, so named because they were built at French Creek on the Allegheny River.

The boats, which were sixty-eight to seventy-nine feet long, sixteen feet wide and four and one-half to five feet deep, had a capacity of four thousand to six thousand bushels of coal. Once loaded, they were floated to Pittsburgh and on down to communities along the Ohio River. Pairs of boats were sometimes lashed together with ropes and fitted up with steering oars and other equipment, along with a crew consisting of a pilot and sixteen men. In May 1841, one H.H. Finley piloted a pair of boats loaded with about six thousand bushels of coal apiece downriver to Cincinnati. He "lost" one boat en route, but in August, he sold the remaining load for five cents per bushel, making a profit of eighty dollars on that particular expedition.

By the late 1830s, coal production was increased by the construction of coal railroads to the mines in the hills and further inland from the river. (Coal railroads were in use long before passenger rail service became generally available.) By 1837, there were thirty-five or forty small railroads in operation in the coalfields between Pittsburgh and Brownsville that had an annual production of twelve million bushels. As the century wore on, the coal mining industry increased steadily. A mine near Greenfield (Coal Center) after the Civil War employed 125 men who were paid at the rate of three and a half cents per bushel. This mine yielded about one million bushels annually. And it was Jonathan Allison who extensively developed the Allison mine near McGovern in the 1870s.

The newly constructed Chartiers Valley Railroad (later the Pennsylvania) provided the means of transportation by which the coal was shipped to the borough of Washington. The Allison mine employed fifty men and produced about five thousand bushels per day. The coal was shipped to Waynesburg, Pittsburgh and as far away as Chicago. Other pioneer coal operators included T. Burr Robbins and Company, Thomas Taylor, G.W. Crawford and J.V.H. Cook, as well as the Locust Grove Mine at Canonsburg and the Brier Hill Mine, operated by J.D. Sanders and Company near McDonald. The completion of the Pittsburgh Southern Railroad in 1879 helped development of the Union Valley Mine and one operated by David M. Anderson, both near Finleyville.

By the 1870s, mining operations had become so extensive that mine safety became a matter of public concern. The Pennsylvania legislature in 1870 passed a law requiring all coal mines to be equipped with a second entrance for reasons of safety and ventilation. The growth of mining operations during the latter part of the nineteenth century provided Washington County with a prosperity boom. Real estate values hit new highs as handsome prices were paid for both surface and coal lands. Prices that began at $16 and $18 per acre increased to $40 and then to $100 per acre; after the turn of the century, they shot up to $250, and by 1910, coal lands near the river were selling for $1,800 per acre.

As mines were often located in remote regions, the company store, owned by the mine, was the shopping and social center of every "coal patch" community. *Courtesy Washington County Historical Society.*

In 1881, there were about thirty coal producers in Washington County. They employed 2,140 miners with an output of 800,162 tons. By 1890, the number of miners had increased to 4,341 and total production reached 2,471,241 tons. In 1900, 6,535 miners increased the production to 4,884,828 tons. Between 1900 and 1907, the number of miners employed jumped to 16,000 and production skyrocketed to 14,545,599 tons.

Some of the dozens of mines in business at the turn of the century included the Pittsburgh-Buffalo Coal Company, the Monongahela Consolidated Coal and Coke Company, the Vesta Coal Company, Ellsworth Collieries Company, Penobscott Coal Company and the Prior Coal Company. They operated mines with interesting names like Jumbo, Primrose, Raccoon, Star, Beaumont, Champion, Diamond, Dandy, Germania and Hazel. In 1907, Washington County ranked fifth in the state in bituminous coal production, and it was in the midst of a forty-year boom; by 1919, the coal business was the largest industry in the county.

The Washington Female Seminary

One of the primary interests of the early settlers in western Pennsylvania was, as we have already noted, the establishment of preparatory schools and colleges. The education of young men for the ministry, medicine and teaching was most important. While the education of girls above the elementary level did not receive immediate attention, it is to the everlasting credit of some of Washington's most influential men that they were among the first in the region to recognize the need for schools of higher learning for their daughters. The old colonial attitude that girls needed no education beyond elementary competence in reading, writing and arithmetic was on the way out by the beginning of the nineteenth century. Catherine Beecher, Mary Lyon and Emma Willard were among the pioneers in the establishment of secondary schools for women in the 1820s and '30s. And in Washington, farsighted men like Alexander Reed and Francis J. LeMoyne were giving the matter of female education their personal attention.

During the month of November 1835, a number of prominent men met at the home of Congressman T.M.T. McKennan to discuss the organization of a school for girls. The group also included Dr. David Elliott, Dr. David McConaughy, Thomas Morgan, John H. Ewing, Dr. Robert R. Reed and many others. They agreed to set up a school for girls and undertook their task with dispatch. The method of financing was simple: shares of stock were sold at $50 each. More than $4,000 was quickly raised; this sum was used to purchase a site and erect a building. Pending construction of the school, classes met in the Masonic Hall; Mrs. Frances Biddle was engaged

The Washington Female Seminary, as it appeared in the 1880s. *From* Caldwell's Atlas.

as principal, and the Washington Female Seminary was in business. In fact, the Pennsylvania legislature chartered the school in April 1836, and the first session began with forty pupils on April 21.

Public examinations of each class, by trustees as well as teachers, were the custom of the day, and the first were held on October 8, 1836. The young ladies insisted that they were nervous and frightened, but they exhibited such knowledge and industry that the trustees and audience were much impressed. The course of study included grammar, ancient and modern geography, mental and natural philosophy, history, arithmetic, astronomy and evidence of Christianity. By that time, the main part of the building had been completed, and boarders were in residence. Yearly rates for tuition were $10.00 for primary, $15.00 for junior and $21.00 for senior students. The charge for board was $1.75 per week.

While the students were industrious and happy and the school appeared to grow, it became apparent that Mrs. Biddle was not quite the person for the job. After four years as principal, she resigned, and the board selected Miss Sarah R. Foster, a former student and a friend of Emma Willard, as the new principal. The board chose well; the new principal was to serve for thirty-four years, and under her expert guidance, the seminary soon became one of the most respected schools for girls in the region. She was a born administrator, possessed of uncommon tact and energy. In no time at all, she and her school began to exercise a great influence on the entire community.

One of the more interesting events of Miss Foster's early administration occurred in 1843. Important travelers were forever stopping off in Washington during these years—the heyday of the National Road. One of those visitors was a congressman from Massachusetts, former president John Quincy Adams, then seventy-six years old. Mr. Adams visited Washington in November 1843, and one of his stops was at the seminary. The *Reporter* covered the event and recorded a curious exchange of remarks between the principal and the former president. In those days, ladies rarely made speeches in public, but the capable Miss Foster became one of the first exceptions. She delivered a brief but gracious public welcome to her guest. The startled Adams replied in his most courtly and gallant fashion. Admitting that this was the first occasion in which a lady had addressed him personally in public, he allowed that he was quite touched by the unexpected honor. So pleased was he at his reception that he promised his best prayers for the success and prosperity of the seminary and all other schools like it.

The good wishes and prayers of President Adams were not in vain. The school flourished and prospered; classes grew in size as Miss Foster recruited talented and capable faculty. By 1845, the curriculum had been expanded to include geology, algebra, geometry, political economy, chemistry, botany, rhetoric, logic, mental and moral science and scripture history. Pupils were assigned to one of three departments—senior, junior or third division—with tuition charges of fourteen, eleven and nine dollars respectively per session. The school year was divided into two five-month sessions, from November to March and from May to September. The nerve-wracking public examinations took place in March and September. The fee for board, lodging and laundry had gone up a bit, to fifty dollars per session, with an additional charge of five dollars for fuel during the winter months.

The hospitable three-story building, which fronted Maiden Street, had forty lodging rooms, a large hall and recitation rooms. The students' rooms were furnished, and the girls were expected to keep them neat and tidy. The furnishings would be regarded as decidedly chilly and austere by today's standards. Carpets could be found only in the parlors and in the teachers' quarters; no pictures adorned the walls, and there was no central heating. Warmth was provided by small coal or wood fires in each room. There was as yet no gas, electricity or running water. Dip tallow candles provided light. Beds were equipped with two mattresses, a straw one for summer and a feather one for winter. Pupils took turns serving as "monitress" and were responsible for visiting the dormitory rooms during study hours to make sure that students were in their rooms if they were supposed to be in or out if they were supposed to be out. Demerits were given for infractions. Food was abundant and apparently good. While life was rugged, letters written by students of the period attest that they found it enjoyable.

The school survived two disasters during Miss Foster's first decade. In 1848, fire destroyed a newly constructed wing of the building, and the emergency created quite a sensation. When the bell in the courthouse tower sounded the alarm, court was hastily adjourned to permit judges, juries, attorneys and citizens to rush to the scene. Three fire companies and a bucket brigade of women, children and schoolgirls all joined in the effort to douse the flames. When the fire was out, the young ladies were placed with families in town, care being taken by the principal to "remove them as far as possible from the temptation of the presence of the masculine element."

The seminary class of 1880. *Courtesy Citizens Library.*

Lower School girls at the maypole. *Courtesy Citizens Library.*

Parade float celebrating the Seminary Centennial in 1936. *Courtesy Citizens Library.*

Another catastrophe occurred in 1850 when an epidemic of scarlet fever forced the school to close briefly. Unfortunately, several pupils died. Another trying time was the Civil War period. However, the school survived these crises with such success that a reunion in honor of the principal's first quarter century of service was held in June 1866. By this time, it was clear that not only was the Washington Seminary firmly established but also that the principle of higher education of women was here to stay. Farsighted alumnae looked forward to the time when girls would be as liberally educated as boys and when all women who wished to do so would be able to prepare for any career they desired.

Thus did the seminary finish its first three decades of service to the Washington community. It had more than lived up to the hopes of its founders and would go on about the business of educating young women for the next eighty years.

Solomon Spaulding

A Mormon Mystery?

Washington County during the past two hundred years has been the setting for more than one little cause célèbre. It was assured of a place in American history books as the scene of the Whiskey Rebellion in the 1790s. Then, in the nineteenth century, there was another interesting controversy—not as violent as the rebellion, but one with national repercussions. This was the Spaulding affair.

It all began innocently enough with the birth of Solomon Spaulding, son of a New England farmer, in Ashford County, Connecticut, in 1761. The child of reasonably affluent parents, in those years before the Revolutionary War, Solomon was well educated and finally dispatched to Dartmouth College, from which he was graduated with honors in 1785. Spaulding then embarked on a career as a preacher, but bad luck seemed to trail him wherever he went. His health was poor, and after three or four years of service as a minister in the Congregationalist Church, he went to Cherry Valley, New York, and set up shop as a merchant. This didn't work out either, and in 1809, he moved his family to Conneaut, Ohio, where he began to operate a forge.

The numerous ancient Indian mounds and fortifications in the Conneaut area so fascinated Spaulding that he determined to write a "romance" that would endeavor to explain the presence of prehistoric mound builders in this part of North America. His investigations were stimulated by a natural interest in literature and history, and the innocent, imaginative chronicle that he labored over for months became a source of entertainment not only for the author but also for an admiring circle of friends and neighbors. In those frontier days, amusements were scarce; books and magazines were also rare, so it was not surprising that Spaulding's neighbors began to look forward with eager anticipation to each succeeding chapter of his novel, which he entitled *Manuscript Found*. The fact that so many people listened with interest to each installment as he read it to them became very significant in later years.

Spaulding's tale was basically an imaginative account of how the prehistoric Indians happened to come to that spot. His story was based on the theme that they were descendants of one of the lost tribes of Israel, who wandered afar, by land and sea, until they came to America. Bloody wars followed, and the burial of the thousands of victims in great heaps explained the presence of the numerous mounds that dotted the Ohio countryside. The adventures of Spaulding's chief characters—Nephi, Laman and Lehi—remained forever in the minds of his audience as they listened to chapter after chapter of his narrative. And they particularly noticed how frequently he began his paragraphs with the Biblical phrase "and it came to pass." Eventually, they even began to refer to the author affectionately as "Old came-to-pass." All in all, Solomon Spaulding's tale made quite an indelible impression on his listeners.

Finally, about 1812, Spaulding decided that since his friends and neighbors were so interested in his historical novel, he would take his manuscript to Pittsburgh, try to get it published and then perhaps live happily ever after on the proceeds. He moved to the city and there entrusted his precious work to a printer named Patterson. Regrettably, the popular manuscript was not published as its author had hoped, either because of reservations on the part of the printer as to whether it would sell or due to a lack of funds on the part of the author to pay for the job. In any case, Spaulding apparently left his manuscript behind and moved with his family to Amity, in Washington County, where in 1814 they settled in a rented house built in 1796 by one Henry Wicks. This dwelling came to have considerable historical importance. Of frame construction, it was the first house of its kind to be built in Amity. And it was built to last, with handmade nails, a walnut stairway, a stone and clay chimney and two large fireplaces. Used in later years as a tavern, post office, storeroom and office, the house became famous because the Spauldings had lived there. It stood until it was razed in 1948.

During the two years in which he lived in Amity, Spaulding ran a tavern in one more effort to become a successful businessman, and he apparently gave up any hope of publishing the manuscript over which he had labored for so long. He died on October 20, 1816, at the age of fifty-five and was buried two days later in a little churchyard in Amity.

It was several years after Spaulding's death that he and his *Manuscript Found* achieved national notoriety in a most curious fashion. During the 1820s, in New York State, one Joseph Smith was busily at work organizing a new religion that in 1830 was formally recognized as the Church of Jesus Christ of Latter-day Saints, or the Mormon Church. It was at this point that Spaulding's "romance," which had been left with Patterson the printer in Pittsburgh several years earlier, became the object of a tug-of-war between the Mormons and a rather large following of Spaulding's friends, relatives and neighbors. Smith claimed that the Book of Mormon was based on information written on a collection of golden plates that he had located after the angel Moroni appeared in a vision and told him where to find them. Spaulding's friends insisted that the book was the manuscript that Spaulding had left in Pittsburgh many years before, and a number of them produced lengthy and detailed testimonials to support their position. Charges and countercharges regarding the authorship of the Book of Mormon have flown back and forth ever since.

An astonishing cast of characters took shape as the controversy developed. First there was the assortment of relatives who were sure that Spaulding's work and the Book of Mormon had a remarkable number of similarities in their historical narratives. Characters of the same name appeared in both works, they had similar adventures and the frequent repetition of Spaulding's favorite phrase "and it came to pass" caused his friends to observe to one another that "old came-to-pass has come to life again." All of this provided some impetus for the theory that Spaulding's narrative had somehow been lifted from Patterson's print shop and made its way to Joseph Smith's headquarters at Palmyra, New York. Two of the persons who supposedly assisted in this deception were Sydney Rigdon, a native of Library, Pennsylvania, who lived in Pittsburgh and frequented Patterson's print shop during the period when Spaulding left his manuscript there and one Parley P. Pratt, a "peddler who knew everybody in western New York and Northern Ohio." Both Rigdon and Pratt were early converts and ministers in the Mormon Church.

A careful account of this interesting controversy, together with testimonials supporting Spaulding and his story, appears within the pages of Boyd Crumrine's *History of Washington County*. Written by Robert Patterson of Pittsburgh, a son of Patterson the printer who originally

Solomon Spaulding's grave marker in Amity cemetery. *Courtesy* Washington Observer-Reporter.

accepted Spaulding's "romance" for possible publication, the account of the alleged deception makes fascinating reading.

So the argument raged. Scholars on both sides have studied the tangled mass of evidence for years. The Mormons, of course, insisted that Spaulding's work bore no resemblance to the Book of Mormon. Obviously, it would have been convenient if Spaulding's original could have been produced to prove or disprove the controversy. Unfortunately, the original disappeared; there was talk that it or a copy had been located, but these claims only added fuel to the dispute. As the years went by, Spaulding's grave in Amity was visited by hundreds of the curious, many of whom walked away with pieces of the tombstone. By 1900, the original marker had disappeared almost entirely. It was replaced in 1905 with a monument bearing the same inscription that appeared on the original. During the heyday of the quarrel, there were even postcards featuring photographs of the Spaulding house in Amity as well as the new granite marker over his grave.

Whatever the truth of the matter, the innocent author of a controversial unpublished manuscript sleeps in a peaceful Amity churchyard while the origin of the Book of Mormon, at least in some quarters, remains a mystery.

THE HANGING ON GALLOWS HILL

The first execution for murder in Washington County was a sensational event that attracted between eight thousand and fifteen thousand spectators to Gallows Hill. (The very first execution took place in 1784, when a horse thief named Thomas Richardson was hanged, probably in the vicinity of the junction between Stokeley Street and Acheson Avenue. This area had the shape of a natural amphitheater; spectators could gather on the hill above and witness the proceedings below.) The year for this second execution was 1823, and the events that led to the hanging on the hill were the result of a family squabble involving one of the most colorful characters ever to cross the Alleghenies.

The crime took place in 1822. William Crawford, nicknamed "Old Britannia," was an elderly eccentric who had been engaged for years in a feud with his twenty-eight-year-old son, Henry. One July day, after completing some farm chores with neighbors who had come by to help, Crawford Sr. invited all hands into the house for a drink of whiskey. During the revelry, the old man complained about his son's torments and vowed that he would kill him if he came around again to make mischief. Some of those in the party took the threat seriously and went out to the barn to alert Henry, who refused to heed the warning. The July day wore on, and evening found Henry sitting on a log near his father's door, singing a song that he knew the old man detested. As Henry began the second verse, Crawford raised his rifle, rested it against the door frame and, taking deliberate aim, shot Henry dead. A justice of the peace was summoned to take Crawford into custody. According to contemporary accounts of the tragedy, the murderer showed no remorse; indeed, he insisted that he had intended to kill Henry and allowed that, if he had to, he would do so again.

By his own admission, William Crawford was a lusty, brawling Irishman, who traced a lifelong contempt for women and a love of money to his early interest in fun and games. Born in County Fermanagh in 1748, he spent a few years in "frolic and sport" before enlisting in the Prince of Wales Regiment of Light Dragoons. In due time, his passion for adventure lured him to Quebec as a member of an infantry regiment. He fought on the British side in the American Revolution under General John Burgoyne. Captured and imprisoned near Martinsburg, Virginia, he engineered an escape for more than sixty men, himself included. Recaptured, he escaped again, this time with the help of the sheriff's daughter, whom he described as a "tall and beautiful girl." Her name was Lydia. They took refuge in a local tavern owned by a captain in the Virginia militia. There they were located the next morning by Lydia's outraged mother. Wedding plans were hastily made, then and there.

According to Crawford, the next five years were the happiest of his life. He settled down as a family man and was even appointed deputy sheriff and keeper of the jail in which he had recently been confined. He bought land and houses in Martinsburg and worked as a stonemason. During this period, he and his wife had two children.

Unfortunately, this interlude of domestic bliss came to an end during the waning days of the Revolutionary War. Crawford was arrested as a traitor and a spy for consorting with Tory sympathizers. His own wife turned him in. English loyalists who wanted to join Lord Cornwallis as that general made his last stand at Yorktown had gotten in touch with Crawford, who really wanted no part of the deal. However, he refused to divulge the names of those who had contacted him and was arrested and released eight to ten times within a two-day period. The authorities could get nothing out of him, and at last he was freed. Quarrels with his wife and her family continued, however, and finally Lydia and the two children left him. Apparently, he never saw them again.

Discouraged and disheartened, Crawford wound up his affairs in Martinsburg and crossed the mountains into western Pennsylvania, where he took up the iron trade. Eventually, he met and set up housekeeping with a woman named Rebecca, who had an unspecified number of children. Their life together was a stormy one, and his relationship with Rebecca's son Henry was particularly troublesome. In spite of their difficulties and conflicts, however, the family remained together for a number of years.

As time went by, Crawford became convinced that Rebecca and the children were out to ruin him. According to Forrest, they interfered with his plans to operate a farm and a still; they teased him and became "drunk, abusive, and pilfering." Crawford and Rebecca were in and out of court as they accused each other of an assortment of misdeeds. Crawford complained that Henry beat him and plotted to kill him and confiscate his property. The old man concluded that he was worse off at home than he had ever been in prison. In short, he felt that he was the victim of persecution. Such was the background for the awful deed in July 1822.

Crawford spent four months in the Washington County jail as he awaited trial on November 21, 1822. An impressive array of legal talent appeared to defend him: James Ross, Parker Campbell, T.M.T. McKennan and John Kennedy. The case was heard before Judge Thomas H. Baird, and the prosecuting attorneys were William Baird and Joseph Pentecost. Thirty-four jurors were called before a panel of twelve could be seated. The case went to the jury the next day, November 22, at 3:20 p.m. By 4:30 p.m., the verdict of "guilty of murder in the first degree" was announced to the assembly in the crowded little courtroom.

Sentence of death by hanging was pronounced on the following morning to a still unrepentant prisoner; after a long address by the judge, in which the crime was described in detail as an "atrocity," the condemned man insisted that he felt no remorse. An appeal to the State Supreme Court was turned down. Crawford was still unmoved and showed almost no emotion. He tried to starve to death but, after several days, had to give in to hunger. Most of his time was spent in writing his memoirs, part of which were published in the *Examiner*, a local newspaper of the period. The execution was scheduled for February 21, 1823.

The case had attracted a great deal of attention throughout the region, hence the throng that assembled on Gallows Hill to witness the grim event. Even the militia had to be called out to help keep order. In the meantime, back at the jail, preparations for transporting the condemned man to the execution site had been completed. The day was snowy, so Crawford was taken through the streets of the town on a sled, riding beside his own coffin. His manner was cheerful, his countenance ruddy, clear and apparently untroubled. He joshed with onlookers as he rode to the hill, peeled an apple, ate it and observed that there was no hurry as the proceedings were not likely to begin until he got there.

His escort included the sheriff, a deputy, several clergymen and members of the militia, who helped to control the crowd. When the party arrived at the gallows, services were conducted by the delegation of ministers. The Baptist preacher, the Reverend Charles Wheeler, begged Crawford to pray and to forgive his enemies. This he refused to do, rebuffing the entreaties with an admonition to the Reverend Mr. Wheeler to mind his own business.

The preliminaries completed, the members of the escort party descended to the ground, leaving the condemned man alone with the sheriff. The two shook hands, and the black cap was drawn over Crawford's eyes. The sheriff picked up a hatchet, whacked the cord that held the trap and the deed was done.

As the years went by, most local executions took place in the jail yard, and the number of spectators was very limited. However, in the 1870s, Gallows Hill once again became famous when Dr. F.J. LeMoyne built the first crematory in the United States on the site.

Therein lies another tale.

THE LEMOYNE HOUSE

Its Role in the Slavery Issue

The history of slavery in Washington County and the Commonwealth of Pennsylvania goes all the way back to William Penn and the original charter which he received from King Charles II in 1681. Slaves came with the first settlers to the colony, and William Penn himself owned slaves. However, the Quakers were opposed to slavery from the beginning, and most of them abhorred its continuation. As early as 1688, efforts were made through the quarterly and yearly meetings of the Society of Friends to discourage slave traffic. William Penn recommended to the Provincial Assembly of Pennsylvania that the slave trade be discontinued, and he provided in his will for the emancipation of his own slaves.

In spite of the agitation by Pennsylvania settlers against the practice, the slave trade was continued throughout the colonial period because the British government refused to suppress it. However, the Quakers continued to press vigorously for its abolition, and by 1776, members of the Society of Friends could not retain membership in the church if they were slaveholders.

Finally, in February 1779, about three years after the Declaration of Independence was signed, the Supreme Executive Council of Pennsylvania recommended legislation that would abolish slavery. The General Assembly agreed and, on March 1, 1780, passed an act that provided for the gradual abolition of slavery throughout the commonwealth. Provisions were such that the practice would disappear within a generation. Pennsylvania became the first of the states to provide for the emancipation of slaves within its jurisdiction. In Washington County, for example, the slave population in

1790 was 263; by 1800, the number had dropped to 84 and, by 1810, the figure was 36.

As slavery gradually passed out of existence in Pennsylvania and in Washington County, many of those concerned with its universal abolition were eager to assist in its extermination on the national level. The American Colonization Society, founded in 1816, led the fight for antislavery legislation for many years. The colonizationists, as they were called, wished to free the slaves and set up a self-governing state for them in a region known as the Grain Coast in western Africa. The American Colonization Society accomplished part of its goal, for in 1822, the Republic of Liberia was founded. Liberia received active support from the society until 1847, when it ceased to be dependent upon the organization. Its constitution was based on that of the United States, which gave it diplomatic recognition in 1862.

However, as the century wore on, slavery seemed to be more entrenched than ever in the United States, especially in the South, even though Congress had passed legislation forbidding slave trade after 1807. William Lloyd Garrison, who founded the American Anti-Slavery Society in 1833, insisted that the American Colonization Society's plan was a failure and that the only way to solve the slavery issue was to work for its complete abolition, immediately and without compensation. Within a few years, the abolitionist movement had spread through the Middle Atlantic states and into the West.

In Washington County, the abolitionist cause found staunch supporters in the county seat and in West Middletown. In fact, Washington County went through a period of turbulence on the slavery issue that had not been equaled since the days of the Whiskey Rebellion forty years earlier. Dr. Francis J. LeMoyne converted to the cause in 1834 after he had read the constitution of the Pennsylvania Anti-Slavery Society, which had been founded in the eighteenth century, long before the national group was organized. The principles to which Dr. LeMoyne subscribed stated plainly that slavery was a violation of human rights, that it was contrary to the spirit of Christianity and that the immediate and unconditional emancipation of slaves was a moral obligation.

The Washington County Anti-Slavery Society was organized on July 4, 1834, and Joseph Henderson served as its first president. By the time the group observed its first anniversary, Dr. LeMoyne was a strong supporter, and he was elected president in 1835. By 1836, the activities of the organization had aroused widespread and sometimes violent community opposition from colonizationists, proslavery advocates and just plain hoodlums.

The uproar reached its height when, in June 1836, the Reverend Samuel Gould, a speaker who was touring the nation on behalf of the abolitionist cause, was scheduled to speak at the Cumberland Presbyterian Church on West Wheeling Street. Rumors of impending trouble had caused Dr. LeMoyne to recruit some sturdy supporters of the free speech movement (another sprouting political party of the day; its supporters were not necessarily antislavery, but they were strongly in favor of free speech). These reinforcements could be counted on to halt the expected troublemakers. Rabble-rousers did indeed appear outside the building, and as one of their number advanced down the aisle of the church, he was confronted by the large, powerful doctor, who stared him down with cold, steely eyes. The intruder decided not to take on Dr. LeMoyne personally, but his hasty departure was the signal for the rioting to begin. Eggs, bricks and stones were hurled through the windows, and the din was such that the speaker could scarcely be heard. At the conclusion of his talk, he was whisked away by sturdy bodyguards.

The group's destination was the LeMoyne house, but the unruly crowd hindered their progress. As they passed the home of Daniel Moore at the corner of West Wheeling and Main, a side door popped open suddenly, a long arm shot out and snatched the Reverend Mr. Gould from the street to safety. His bodyguard tumbled in also, and the group exited by way of the front door on South Main Street, thus giving the jeering crowd the slip for a few moments. Finally, they made it to the safety of Dr. LeMoyne's stone house. The mob continued to riot for some time before it finally dispersed.

A public meeting was held later in the month at which various burgesses of Washington Borough deplored the whole affair. They passed a resolution suggesting that it would be unwise for members of the abolitionist society to continue to intrude their "peculiar and offensive doctrines" on the people of the county. Undaunted by the mob or the borough council, Dr. LeMoyne and the Anti-Slavery Society determined to hold their annual July 4 meeting at the doctor's house, with the intrepid Reverend Mr. Gould again the featured speaker. Since violence was anticipated, Dr. LeMoyne once more recruited a dozen or so brawny advocates of the free speech movement. They were stationed in front of the house, armed with stout hickory clubs. And up on the long front balcony of the house, where beehives had replaced Dr. John LeMoyne's conservatory, his eight-year-old grandson was stationed with a long pole with instructions to dislodge one of the hives on any rioters

The LeMoyne House, ca. 1862. A National Historic Landmark, the LeMoyne home on Maiden Street, Washington, was a center of antislavery activity and an important stop on the Underground Railroad. It now houses the Washington County Historical Society. *Courtesy Ray W. Forquer, artist, and Countryside Prints, Inc.*

who might break through the line of guards. The meeting in the yard on the east side of the big house proceeded peacefully enough, somewhat to the disappointment of the young sentinel on the balcony. A few hecklers did appear but decided against intrusion when they beheld the menacing guards armed with clubs. Serious opposition melted completely when one confused rioter, upon hearing a speaker read from the Declaration of Independence that "all men are created equal," decided that it was abolitionist propaganda and yelled, "Stop; we don't want to hear any more of that—stuff!" With that, the demonstration collapsed and the rioters dispersed.

Dr. LeMoyne continued to be one of the strongest abolitionists in western Pennsylvania. He was on three occasions—in 1841, 1844 and 1847—the unsuccessful candidate of the Liberty (abolitionist) Party for governor of Pennsylvania. The failure of the Liberty Party to carry much weight in national or state elections led to its merger in 1848 with the Free Soil Party

("Free soil, free speech, free labor and free men".) This party enjoyed modest success in winning several House and Senate seats in Congress, but by 1856, it had merged with the newly organized Republican Party.

Meantime, back in Washington County, the slavery issue was anything but dead. In the 1840s and 1850s, as we shall see, the abolitionists increased their activities, and an effective underground railroad network was soon established in southwestern Pennsylvania.

ABOLITIONISTS AND THE
UNDERGROUND RAILROAD

For those who are fascinated by intrigue and mystery, there has probably been nothing before or since to equal the suspense-filled days just before the Civil War, when many people in Washington County were busily involved with the Underground Railroad. The activities of Dr. Francis J. LeMoyne and the Anti-Slavery Society during the 1830s have already been described. While Dr. LeMoyne and his friends were recruiting abolitionist supporters in the county seat, certain people in West Middletown were already hard at work for the same cause.

Although slavery was fast disappearing from the scene in western Pennsylvania during the first quarter of the nineteenth century, there were many who wished to hasten its extinction at the national level. Antislavery societies were formed in several places in Washington County, and among the most active were those in Washington and West Middletown. An Abolition Society was in existence in West Middletown as early as 1827. One of its most vigorous supporters was William McKeever, who had long been a prominent citizen of the community.

West Middletown, founded just before the turn of the nineteenth century, was basically a tranquil but nevertheless extremely busy little village. Its citizens worked hard, and the industrious community on the ridge midway between Washington and Wellsburg served as a convenient stopping place for pioneers headed west. The inhabitants valued religious training and education as important to their young; thus churches and schools were a vital part of community life.

One day in 1830, however, a jolting incident occurred that was to have a far-reaching effect on this God-fearing and independent little village. A group of slaves, worn and weary and chained together, was herded through the main street of the little community. The sight was too much for the abolitionists in the vicinity, and it had a particularly electrifying effect on William McKeever. Outraged by the injustice of it all and the manner in which the owners flogged and cursed their charges, he confronted the procession and publicly denounced the slave drivers. They urged him to back off, but he continued to heap wrathful denunciations upon them and even dared them to shoot him. The whole sorry episode ended without local violence, but the fever of abolitionist sentiment in West Middletown burned more fiercely than ever.

The issue of fugitive slaves had long been a problem at the national level. As early as 1793, Congress had passed a slave law permitting owners to recover their property simply by presenting proof of ownership to a magistrate. Captured slaves were then returned to their masters without benefit of a jury trial or the privilege of giving evidence on their own behalf. By the mid-nineteenth century, the 1793 law was no longer in effect, but one of the provisions of the Compromise of 1850 included hefty penalties to be levied against those who helped runaway slaves to escape.

Some northern states, where abolitionists were particularly active, retaliated by passing laws providing stiff penalties for state and local officials who tried to enforce the federal fugitive slave laws. Even so, Dr. LeMoyne in Washington and the McKeevers in West Middletown pursued their abolitionist activities at considerable personal risk from federal prosecution. Such was the secrecy involved that, as late as 1882, Crumrine wrote that it was still too early "to make known the names of persons who assumed the responsibility of caring for and aiding these fugitives…they might be subjected to the reflections of those who think that a law, however wrong, should be obeyed until repealed." And yet, during this dangerous period, there were numerous "gentlemen of good position who were always ready to aid fugitives from slavery."

Meantime, back in West Middletown, both Thomas and Matthew McKeever supported their father in the abolitionist movement. By the 1850s, the brothers (their father died in 1838) received support from a very important person—none other than John Brown himself. Brown had long been associated with Matthew McKeever in the sheep business, so it was not surprising that he frequently found it necessary to come to West Middletown on sheep-buying expeditions. He was often a visitor in Matthew McKeever's

Abolitionist John Brown and Matthew McKeever were personal friends; Brown was a frequent visitor at their home. *Historical sketch courtesy McKeever Study Library, West Middletown.*

house. In spite of the fact that the federal penalties were severe for those who helped slaves escape, the brothers helped to develop in western Pennsylvania a network of underground "stations" that became very effective in assisting hundreds of slaves in their flight northward to Canada and freedom.

The fugitives crossed the Mason-Dixon line at Crowe's Mills on the line between Virginia and Greene County, Pennsylvania. Friendly farms sheltered them along Wheeling Creek and on the road to Graysville in northern Greene County. Three hours away was another friendly farm at West Alexander. The route then took them to West Middletown twelve miles away. Here, in one of the most famous of all stations in Pennsylvania, there were many shelters available. The fugitives were usually transported at night, concealed in wagons under grain, hay or other farm products, including animals. (There were many southern sympathizers in this border country, and the "conductors" on the railroads might encounter enemies as well as friends; hence the stealthy journeys by night.)

Hiding places included barns, cellars, churches and small rooms concealed beneath trap doors in farmhouse kitchens or even in large stone chimneys. Ravines and secluded clearings were also available for shelter. Penitentiary

Woods, about a mile from West Middletown, was a thickly wooded area with a small clearing in the middle. Here a cabin had been built, and a few crops were cultivated. This was such a secluded spot that fugitives sometimes stayed on through the harvest season to lend a helping hand with the fall chores. Matthew McKeever's home, Pleasant Hill, was also the site of a popular seminary operated by his wife, Mrs. Jane Campbell McKeever. One story goes that the boarders at the school, unaware of the undercover activities on the McKeever property, were often encouraged to have songfests and sing-alongs as a device to cover any noisy preparations necessary for the concealment of the fugitives.

McKeever wrote in 1880 about some of his adventures as a conductor with the Underground Railroad. He transported his charges in a spring wagon with a chicken coop on both ends and the fugitives in the middle. A cover over the whole thing concealed the human cargo from view. For one four-week period, a party of eight slaves was kept in the sheep loft.

Above, left: A youthful Dr. LeMoyne. Park Burroughs, artist. *Courtesy* Washington Observer-Reporter.

Above, right: Madeleine LeMoyne strongly endorsed her husband's abolitionist views. Once, it is said, she feigned illness and hid seven escaping slaves under her bed while slave trackers searched the rest of the house. She gambled that they would not disturb a lady in her bedroom. *Courtesy* Washington Observer-Reporter.

McKeever insisted that a hired man managed to feed and care for them without arousing the suspicions of the eighteen to twenty members of the regular household. Even Mrs. McKeever was not aware of the presence of the extra boarders. McKeever figured that he helped to ship thirty-five to forty slaves northward to freedom.

In Washington, the LeMoyne house was also an important station. Mrs. Madeleine LeMoyne Reed recalled that her father had given refuge to as many as twenty-five fugitives at one time in a secret room on the third floor of the big stone mansion on Maiden Street. And many were the tales of black lookouts who served as undercover agents and runners. One went around on crutches on West Chestnut Street in Washington. When he spotted slave hunters riding into town, he immediately discarded his disguise and took off at top speed to warn those who were concealing his brethren in West Middletown. Another helpful black in Wheeling hid many a slave until he could be safely transported to the next station. After the war, this "conductor" settled in West Middletown where he was provided with land and a house by friendly neighbors.

The number of slaves who achieved freedom via the Underground Railroad through Ohio and Pennsylvania finally ran into the thousands. There can be little doubt that the heroic efforts of the LeMoynes, the McKeevers and their supporters in Washington County contributed greatly to the success of the operation.

THE WASHINGTON INVINCIBLES

In April 1861, civil war burst upon a stricken nation. After decades of turmoil concerning a number of political, economic and social problems, one compromise after another failed to resolve slavery, the overriding emotional issue that finally blew the nation apart. In 1861, there were thirty-four states in the Union, with more to come, and the admission of each new state created further controversy as to whether it should be admitted as a free or a slave state. Sticky sectional quarrels regarding tariffs and states' rights could not be resolved. The industrial northeast and the growing west generally lined up against an agricultural south, whose economy depended to a great extent on the availability of slave labor. By the spring of 1861, scarcely a month after Lincoln's inauguration, ominous talk of secession was heard across the land. Thus another and more dangerous element was added to the growing list of problems that beset the United States just seventy years after it joined the family of nations. The Union would have to be preserved—but how?

The die was cast when, on Friday, April 12, 1861, Confederate batteries circling Charleston harbor fired on the Federal forces at Fort Sumter. On Monday, April 15, President Lincoln issued a proclamation declaring the South to be in a state of rebellion and calling for seventy-five thousand volunteers to help put it down. In Washington County, the response was immediate. The first volunteer to enlist in Washington was James B. Kennedy. Within five days, companies from Monongahela and Washington were organized and set to go.

Saturday, April 20, dawned with an air of festivity in Little Washington. Most of the population of 3,500 was up early, since departure ceremonies were scheduled to begin at 8:00 a.m. so that Company E, dubbed the "Washington Invincibles," could be on its way by 9:00 a.m. Flag-bedecked streets and buildings, with martial music filling the air, belied an undercurrent of anxiety as wives and mothers made ready to bid farewell to husbands and sons. The volunteers had signed up for three months under this initial call, but a sense of foreboding underlay all the preparations. After all, nobody really knew just what to expect.

Well before the appointed hour, the little public square in front of the courthouse was a mass of densely packed humanity. Members of Company E formed ranks and marched up and down Main Street a time or two before halting in front of the assembled throng. The ladies of the town presented the unit with a beautiful silk flag, and each man received a personal copy of the New Testament.

Robert H. Koontz delivered a touching farewell speech. H.A. Purviance, who accepted the flag on behalf of the entire company, gave the response. With considerable emotion, he declared, "We have lived under this flag in happiness and society; we will defend it in trial and if need be, we will die rather than see it trail in dishonor." After Dr. Brownson had invoked the blessing of God on the "distracted country" and begged his protection for those who were about to depart, the whole assembly then escorted the company to "the head of town" at the corner of Main and Walnut Streets. There the recruits climbed aboard wagons provided by the community and set off for Pittsburgh. By 9:00 a.m., they were on their way. A broadside printed by the *Reporter* and *Tribune, Review and Examiner* on April 22, 1861, listed ninety volunteers who signed up to serve with the Washington Invincibles. Norton McGiffin, captain; William F. Templeton, first lieutenant; Samuel T. Griffith, second lieutenant; and O.R. McNary, first sergeant, led the company. En route to Pittsburgh, Company E was joined by a unit from Canonsburg. Along with Company G from Monongahela, they all became a part of the Twelfth Pennsylvania Regiment. The Monongahela outfit was led by Robert F. Cooper, captain; John S. McBride, first lieutenant; Jesse C. Taylor, second lieutenant; and William W. Thompson, first sergeant. When the Washington Invincibles joined other units of the Twelfth in Pittsburgh, Norton McGiffin was elected lieutenant colonel of the regiment.

Not only did Washington County men volunteer in substantial numbers, but citizens from all over also began early to organize for the war effort. On the same afternoon that the Invincibles departed for Pittsburgh, a large group of men met at the courthouse at 2:00 p.m. "to consider the state of the government and take such action as they might judge expedient to maintain inviolate the supremacy of the constitution and the laws."

The group, assembled on very short notice, took note of the universal sentiment of patriotism and enthusiasm inspired by the events of the last few days. Group members wished to advise and consult with one another about the impending dangers facing the country. An overflow crowd stood in the courtroom and listened solemnly as Colonel W.M. Hopkins, who had been elected president, addressed them on this unprecedented crisis in the nation's history. He urged his listeners to put aside personal and political differences in order to help preserve the Union. The assembly then heard resolutions from a committee chaired by William McKennan.

The report declared that the inhabitants of Washington County, "responding to the proclamation of the President of the United States, hereby declare our unalterable determination to sustain the government in its efforts to maintain the honor, the integrity, and the existence of the National Union." To this end, they promised "to stand together in vindication of our flag" and resolved that the "gallant band of brave volunteers have our heartfelt prayers for preservation and safe return." The meeting broke up with a rousing, "Three cheers for the Union and three cheers for Capt. McGiffin and his gallant band."

The Civil War Soldiers Monument, Washington Cemetery. *Photogravure from* The Art of Washington County.

Company E, along with the rest of the Twelfth Regiment, left Pittsburgh on April 24 and spent its three months' enlistment guarding the Northern Central Railroad between Baltimore and Harrisburg. The first Civil War casualty from Washington County was Private Samuel B. Hickey, a student from Washington College, who became ill and died on July 20, 1861. His body was returned for burial with full military honors in

Washington Cemetery. The rest of the unit was mustered out of service at Harrisburg on August 5, 1861. When the veterans of Company E returned to Washington after their brief and uneventful tour of duty, the citizens turned out to welcome them home. The celebration was not a very jolly one, however, for many of the men immediately signed up for a three-year tour of duty with Company A of the 100th Regiment (the Round Heads) that was being organized. The Round Heads got their nickname because many of the recruits in the 100th were among the descendants of the Covenanters and the men who had followed Cromwell.

The 100th Regiment eventually saw plenty of action at the second Battle of Bull Run (where Captain William F. Templeton, for whom the local G.A.R. post was named, was killed in action), South Mountain, Vicksburg, the Wilderness and Cold Harbor. In addition, other Washington County units served with the 79th, 85th and 140th Regiments. The 79th, which included one company from Washington County, participated in the campaigns at Chickamauga and Atlanta and marched with General Sherman from Atlanta to the sea. The 85th Regiment included three companies of Washington County men; it spent most of its time in Virginia and the Carolinas and ended the war on duty at Richmond and Appomattox. Five companies from Washington County served with the 140th Regiment in the Army of the Potomac and took part in the Battles of Chancellorsville and Gettysburg.

In addition to these infantry regiments, Washington County men also served in two reserve regiments, four cavalry regiments and the Sixth Regiment of Militia. All of the military units were well served by numerous volunteer groups on the home front that made astonishing contributions to the war effort. There is more to be told about Washington County and its determination to help preserve the Union during the tragic days of the "War of the Rebellion."

THE FIGHTING MEN OF RINGGOLD

In addition to the infantry units from Washington County that served during the Civil War, a number of cavalry companies also saw plenty of action. Perhaps the most famous were the companies that made up the Ringgold Battalion. The officer who took the initiative in organizing the outfit was Captain John Keys, a physician who was practicing in Beallsville at the outbreak of the war. A graduate of Jefferson Medical College, Dr. Keys, who was born near Brownsville, settled first in Bentleyville and then in Beallsville. It was while he lived in Bentleyville that he first joined the Ringgold Cavalry. A popular man, enthusiastic about military service, he was soon elected captain of the company.

The Ringgold Cavalry Company had been organized in eastern Washington County following the Mexican War on July 4, 1847. No sooner had President Lincoln issued a call for volunteers in April 1861, than Dr. Keys, as captain of the company, offered the services of his unit to the governor of Pennsylvania.

At that time, the U.S. Secretary of War, Simon Cameron, was for some reason not interested in recruiting cavalry companies, and Captain Keys's offer was turned down not once but twice. Undaunted, he next made a personal appeal to Secretary Cameron, whose father he had known when the elder Cameron worked with Keys's father as a contractor on the National Road. A personal letter to Secretary Cameron got results, with a telegram notifying Keys to report with his unit at once to Grafton, Virginia, to be mustered in. The delighted captain set off on June 22, 1861, from Beallsville with seventy men. They stopped at Carmichaels and then at Morgantown; at both places, they were hospitably received and entertained. Upon reaching Grafton on the twenty-fourth, the unit was outfitted with supplies. Five days later, on June 29, it was mustered into service for a term of three years or for the duration of the war. The Ringgold Company always claimed to be the first volunteer cavalry outfit to be mustered into service.

Keys's unit, designated as Company A, was soon joined by six additional companies from Washington County: Company B, originally known as the Washington Cavalry, was commanded by Captain Andrew J. Greenfield; Company C, the Keystone Cavalry, was commanded

Captain John Keys, leader of the Ringgold Battalion. *Courtesy Washington Observer-Reporter.*

by Captain George F. Work; Company D, the Beallsville Cavalry, was commanded by Captain Harvey H. Young; Company E, the Independent Cavalry, was commanded by Captain Milton W. Mitchener; Company F, the Patton Cavalry, was commanded by Captain Andrew J. Barr; and Company G, known as the Lafayette Cavalry, was commanded by Captain Alexander V. Smith.

All seven companies were soon organized into the Ringgold Cavalry Battalion and placed under the command of Captain Keys, the popular commanding officer of Company A. The battalion saw service in Virginia, Maryland and what is now West Virginia. Most of the time it was employed in scouting, picket duty, marches and raids.

In February 1864, the Ringgold battalion was merged with another battalion into the Twenty-second Pennsylvania Cavalry. The new outfit was assigned to duty in Virginia, Maryland and the Washington, D.C., area. The units were mustered out of service between April and October 1865. Captain Keys, unfortunately, was not among those mustered out; he had died at his Beallsville home in November 1863 as the result of an illness contracted at the front.

Other cavalry units from Washington County served in the First Pennsylvania Cavalry that was made up of companies from a number of counties. Company I, under the command of Captain William H.

The Ringgold Battalion in Pursuit. Courtesy Ray W. Forquer, artist, and Countryside Prints, Inc.

McNulty, was made up entirely of Washington County men. Company K, commanded by Captain William Boyce, included men from both Washington and Allegheny Counties. The First Cavalry served in Virginia on the Rappahannock and in the Shenandoah Valley. It saw plenty of action at the second battle of Bull Run, as well as at Fredericksburg, New Hope Church and Malvern Hill. The regiment was mustered out of service in September 1864.

The Fourteenth Cavalry Regiment included Company H, an outfit made up entirely of Washington County men and commanded by Captain John J. Shutterly of Canonsburg. This regiment saw action in Maryland, Virginia and West Virginia. At the end of the war, the regiment spent a few weeks in Washington, D.C., and in June 1865, it was ordered to Fort Leavenworth. Kansas. There the men were mustered out of service in August 1865.

The Sixteenth Cavalry Regiment included Company K, commanded by Captain Robert W. Parkinson from Washington County. It saw action in the battles of Chancellorsville, Gettysburg, the Wilderness and Malvern Hill. It served briefly in Virginia and North Carolina after the war, guarding captured supplies and preserving order and was mustered out of service in August 1865.

Some of the heaviest fighting involved the two Pennsylvania reserve regiments that included companies of Washington County men. The organization of the reserves was recommended by Governor Curtin in a message to the legislature on April 30, 1861: "to furnish ready support to those who have gone out and to protect our borders…I recommend the immediate organization of at least fifteen regiments of cavalry and infantry, exclusive of those called into the service of the United States." The legislature concurred and ordered the organization of a "Reserve Volunteer Corps of the Commonwealth," which included thirteen infantry regiments and one each of cavalry and light artillery.

The 8th Reserve Regiment in which Company K, commanded by Captain Alexander Wishart, served was ordered to Camp Wilkins, near Pittsburgh, in June 1861. The 8th saw action at Mechanicsville, Gaines Mill, South Mountain, Antietam and Fredericksburg. In February 1863, it was ordered to join the other reserve regiments in the defenses around Washington, D.C. Ordered to the front again with the Army of the Potomac, the regiment was in action at the Wilderness and Spottsylvania. At the end of its three-year period of enlistment, the reenlisted veterans and new recruits were assigned to the 191st Regiment, and the remainder of the 8th was mustered out of service.

The 10th Reserve Regiment included the Jefferson Light Guard (Company D), a unit from Canonsburg under the command of Captain James T. Kirk. It also was ordered to Camp Wilkins near Pittsburgh in June 1861 and served in most of the same campaigns as the 8th Reserves. However, the 10th saw action at Gettysburg while the 8th did not. The 10th arrived at the Gettysburg battle scene on the morning of July 2 and was ordered into the fight at Little Round Top. For the remainder of its three-year period of enlistment, the 10th was on railroad guard duty in Virginia or in action at the Wilderness and Spottsylvania. At the conclusion of the enlistment period, the reenlisting veterans and recruits were assigned to the 190th and 191st regiments while the remainder were mustered out of service.

It is interesting to note that, in connection with the Confederate campaign at Gettysburg during the summer of 1863, there was real concern in June that Confederate forces might very well raid Pittsburgh. Edwin M. Stanton, the secretary of war, notified Major General W.T.H.

Brooks at Pittsburgh on June 10 that enemy intelligence implied that "Pittsburgh will certainly be the point aimed at by Stuart's raid, which may daily be expected. You should frankly inform the people of Pittsburgh that they must be at work."

Stuart did not invade after all, but on June 15, Governor Curtin was warned, "There is not a moment to be lost. The Rebels are moving in large force, and invasion cannot be checked except by immediate action." This time, Lee's army did invade, and the tragic Battle of Gettysburg was the result. The Union and Confederate armies engaged in a deadly conflict that resulted in more than forty thousand casualties on both sides. Lee's retreat from Gettysburg coincided with the fall of the Southern stronghold of Vicksburg to Grant's armies on July 4. It was the beginning of the end for the Confederacy.

WASHINGTON PREPARES FOR INVASION DURING THE CIVIL WAR

The Washington County home front during the Civil War was a very busy scene indeed. Practically everybody was personally involved in one way or another. To supplement the reserves and regular army units, two companies of militia, many of whose members were well past the military age, were briefly in active service as part of the Sixth Regiment of Pennsylvania Militia. During the late summer of 1862, the southern boundary of Pennsylvania was particularly vulnerable to attack by the Confederates, fresh from victory after the second Battle of Bull Run. They had crossed the Potomac into Maryland and were poised for an invasion of the rich harvest fields of the Keystone State. Since Governor Curtin's reserve regiments had been deployed to help General McClellan in Virginia, it fell to the state's militia units to repulse the expected invasion. On September 4, Governor Curtin issued a proclamation calling on the people throughout the commonwealth to prepare for defense. All businesses were to close daily at 3:00 p.m. in order to give newly formed companies and regiments time to practice drills and formations and to receive instruction. By September 10, the governor expected the militia units to be ready to move on an hour's notice. On the following day, the governor, with the approval of President Lincoln, issued a call for fifty thousand men to await orders to march.

In Washington, two companies of the Sixth Militia were mustered into service on September 13. The units were dispatched immediately to Chambersburg, where they joined ten thousand other militiamen camped nearby. An additional twenty-five thousand men were waiting near Harrisburg, ready to move south if their services were needed. On September 17, cannon fire could be heard in the distance. It came from the Antietam battlefield in the vicinity of Sharpsburg, Maryland, where on that hot summer day, the Confederate armies were turned back across the Potomac River into Virginia. This emergency over, the militia units were sent home without taking part in any military action at all.

All remained more or less serene on the home front until the spring of 1863. Then, on June 14, Little Washington was advised of a threatened invasion and ordered to prepare accordingly. Several officers who were at home on furlough or sick leave helped the citizens to mobilize. Units were to report to Washington, where they would be provided with arms, ammunition and other supplies. One of the invasions was supposed to be led by the notorious Confederate raider General John H. Morgan.

Reports reached the nervous citizens that Morgan was planning to strike at Pittsburgh from West Virginia by way of Waynesburg and Washington. People in both communities hastened to set up patrols and assign guards to warn of the Confederates' approach. The organization of patrols was somewhat haphazard, with the result that some of the parties involved did not know where other units were located. This led to confusion, complications and at least one embarrassing incident. One night, when a Washington patrol was checking a road near Waynesburg, they suddenly spotted a party of horsemen just ahead. Without waiting to check the identity of the group, the Washington party took off at top speed toward Waynesburg, yelling, "Morgan is coming!" with every gallop of the horses' hooves. Without stopping in Waynesburg, they continued at full tilt all the way to Washington, spreading the alarm throughout the countryside.

Many panicky citizens took to the hills in self-defense, and it was alleged that some members of the patrol never stopped until they reached Canada. There was plenty of chagrin to go around after the uproar had subsided. What the Washington group had taken for a party of Morgan's men was in reality just a troop of Waynesburg sentinels returning from patrol. According to some reports, it was many a year before the Washington men heard the last of the exciting tale of how they foiled "Morgan's raid on Waynesburg."

While all this excitement was going on, others on the home front were not idle. At the beginning of the war, the federal government was unprepared to supply and equip the thousands of men suddenly called to active duty. Money and basic necessities were urgently needed. The United States Christian Commission was soon organized to help soldiers in the field. In Washington County, its activities were under the direction of Colin M.

Reed. To him fell the responsibility of soliciting contributions from every township, village and neighborhood within the county. Churches sponsored all kinds of events—festivals, fairs and varied entertainments that involved people of all ages—to raise money.

It was estimated that during the four years of the war, the people of Washington County contributed a total of $150,000 in money and supplies toward the war effort; all this was in addition, Crumrine observed, to the "special burdens of taxation incident to the war, and this fact will ever remain as an enduring monument to the generosity and patriotism" of the citizens of Washington County. Clothing and other supplies were desperately needed, and the Ladies' Aid Society of Washington County made significant contributions to this war effort. Organized during the early months of the war by Mrs. Joseph Henderson and Mrs. John L. Gow, the group collected vast quantities of clothing, medicines, wines, bandages and other supplies, which were carefully packed and forwarded to various hospitals in the fields. Among other things, the ladies knitted more than three thousand pairs of woolen socks for which the state paid twenty-five cents per pair. This money was then placed in a fund to be used for the relief of destitute families of soldiers from Washington County. The group was gratified to learn, in a letter of thanks from the Quartermaster-General of Pennsylvania, that its record was unsurpassed by any other county in the commonwealth.

During 1865, the last year of the war, another group called the Ladies Christian Commission of Washington collected $1,082.40, of which $100.00 was donated for a soldiers' monument and $57.40 was given for the improvement of the soldiers' lot in the cemetery; the remaining $925.00 was spent on supplies such as shirts, socks, pillows, linens and wines.

At long last, after four years of struggle and sacrifice, the cruel war was over. On July 4, 1865, the citizens of Washington County organized a gigantic welcome home celebration. The daylong festivities, which included a parade and a picnic, were free to all county soldiers and any other Civil War veterans who happened to be in the vicinity. All citizens were assessed a small sum to cover expenses. Arrangements for the grand affair were under the direction of a special committee, with subcommittees set up in boroughs and townships. The ceremonies got under way at 10:00 a.m., when the procession, with Major John H. Ewing as chief marshal, was organized at the courthouse. Led by veterans of the War of 1812, the parade included 436 veterans from the Washington vicinity and 118 from the Monongahela area. The parade route led down Main to Chestnut, then to Shirls Grove, where Colin M. Reed was elected chairman for the day and ceremonies got

The Pennsylvania Monument erected on the battlefield at Gettysburg. *Courtesy* Washington Observer-Reporter.

under way. A two-hour program included the opening prayer by Dr. James I. Brownson, a reading of the Declaration of Independence, numerous musical selections and several speeches. All of this was followed by a picnic lunch at 1:30 p.m.

Those who did not return were not forgotten. Shortly after the Battle of Gettysburg, a group of citizens began to solicit contributions of $1 each toward the erection of a monument in the cemetery to perpetuate the memory of the Washington County men who lost their lives during the Civil War. Erected in the summer of 1871 at a cost of about $6,000, the monument of Ohio sandstone was topped by an infantry soldier standing at rest and flanked by four Civil War cannon. The forty-one-foot-high monument stands today as a reminder to all who visit of the supreme sacrifice made by the sons of Washington County during the War of the Rebellion.

THE AMITY VOLUNTEERS

The Civil War period remains one of the most tragic and poignant in the nation's history. Even as the country was torn apart, so were families and communities. The extent of the sacrifices offered and the brave deeds performed may be illustrated by a closer examination of one of the Pennsylvania infantry regiments. The 140th Pennsylvania Volunteers served faithfully from 1862 until 1865 and compiled a most honorable history. It was an outfit composed entirely of men from western Pennsylvania; five companies were recruited from Greene, Beaver and Mercer Counties. The other five—companies C, D, E, G and K—were made up of Washington County men.

The little village of Amity provided most of the recruits for Company D, the Ten Mile Infantry. There, Silas Parker, a respected fifty-one-year-old school teacher and justice of the peace, called for volunteers to join him in organizing a unit just after President Lincoln issued a call for three hundred thousand men in the summer of 1862. Under the leadership of Parker, who was elected captain; James Mannon, first lieutenant; and Matthias Minton, second lieutenant, ninety-eight men from Prosperity, West Bethlehem, Washington and even some from Greene County flocked to Amity to join up. With the company went two of the captain's own sons, one of them under eighteen years of age. Captain Parker left his wife in charge of the household and several younger children. Another enlistee, Philo Paul, left his farm, his wife and nine small children. With the unit, when it moved on to the county seat in August, were twelve sets of brothers in addition to the two Parkers.

The Amity Volunteers. Captains George M. Laughlin, Alexander Sweeney and David Acheson posed for this photo in Falmouth, Virginia, in the fall of 1863. *Courtesy Washington and Jefferson College.*

Company C, the Brady Infantry, was organized in Washington by twenty-two-year-old David Acheson, a student at Washington College. Two of his friends, Isaac Vance and Charles Linton, helped with the recruiting. Acheson was elected captain; Vance and Linton were chosen as first and second lieutenants respectively. Companies C and D were soon joined in Washington by Company K, the Reed infantry from Cross Creek, under the command of Captain William A.T. Stockton. These three outfits rendezvoused in Washington and made preparations to travel to Pittsburgh to join other companies that were to be mustered into the regiment.

One day in early September, a large crowd assembled in front of the courthouse to witness the departure ceremonies. Numerous patriotic and emotional speeches were delivered, and a flag was presented to the Brady Infantry by the Reverend Hiram Miller of the Methodist Episcopal Church. The ladies of Amwell Township presented a flag to the Ten Mile Infantry, while Captain Parker and Lieutenants Mannon and Minton received beautiful swords. Captain Stockton of the Reed Infantry was also presented with a handsome sword.

All three companies then set off by wagon for Pittsburgh where, at Camp Howe, they were outfitted and equipped. Presently, they were joined by the other two Washington County units. Company E, which had been organized at Monongahela, was under the command of Captain Aaron Gregg. Captain John Fraser, professor of Mathematics at Jefferson College, was in command of Company G, the Brown Amity Guards. This unit had been named in honor of Dr. Alexander B. Brown, beloved former president of the college. It was Professor Fraser who had told his solemn students at the end of the summer session in 1862, "Young gentlemen—this is our last hour of recitation together. The country needs strong and brave defenders, and since I am sound in wind and limb, I see no good reason why I should not enroll myself with them. After the exercises of Commencement Day, I shall make the attempt to enlist a company from this town and its vicinity."

The professor was as good as his word, and as Captain Fraser, he stood with his men in the Jefferson College Chapel where the sad but proud citizens assembled to send them off to join their comrades in Pittsburgh. Speeches were delivered by prominent speakers, and each recruit received a New Testament. After the ceremonies, the company marched down Central Avenue to Pike Street and on out to Greenside Avenue, where they boarded the wagons and carriages that took them to Pittsburgh. Before the war was over, 35 of the 103 recruits were killed in battle or died of disease.

From Camp Howe, the five Washington County companies journeyed to Camp Curtin near Harrisburg. The other five western Pennsylvania companies from Beaver, Greene and Mercer Counties joined them on September 8; the organization was then officially designated as the 140th Regiment of Pennsylvania Volunteers. On September 9, the regiment moved out of Harrisburg after receiving knapsacks, haversacks, muskets and forty rounds of cartridge ammunition per man. For the next several months, it was posted near Baltimore to keep open the line of the Northern Central Railroad.

In the spring of 1863, the men of the 140th had their baptism of fire in the battle of Chancellorsville during the first week in May. June found the regiment with the Army of the Potomac, and on July 2, it was in the thick of the fighting at Gettysburg. At the Peach Orchard and in the Wheatfield, it was in the midst of terrific and bloody fighting. During this battle, the 140th lost its regimental commander, Colonel Richard P. Roberts, as well as Second Lieutenant Alexander M. Wilson of Company G and Captain David Acheson of Company C. Of all the 588 officers and men present on July 2, the 140th Regiment lost 241, including those wounded and killed in action. Captain Fraser of Company G succeeded Colonel Roberts as regimental commander. Captured by the enemy in November 1864, Fraser rejoined his unit upon his release several months later with the rank of brevet brigadier general.

The news of Captain Acheson's death shocked Washington. "We have never seen our community so startled and overwhelmed with grief," editorialized the *Reporter* on July 15, 1863. It told how Captain Acheson on Thursday, July 2, had heroically led his men "into the storm of fire…how fierce the danger was at that crisis may be inferred from the heavy losses which were sustained by the whole regiment…it was after a large proportion of his men had been disabled, and closely following the severe wounding of his First Lieutenant…that a shot pierced the noble breast of Captain Acheson…it was not until Saturday that his dead body was found." The body of the gallant captain was brought to Washington for burial, and ceremonies took place on Sunday, August 9, 1863. Of the thirty-eight men of Captain Acheson's company who were engaged in action on that hot July afternoon, only five escaped without injury.

After Gettysburg, the 140th fought in the Wilderness, where it suffered more severe losses. It was also present at Cold Harbor, where it lost another sixty men. The regiment took part in the grueling final campaigns at Petersburg and Appomattox. After the war was over, it served briefly in Virginia before moving on the national capital, where the men were mustered out of service on May 31, 1865.

Like Captain Acheson, the courageous Captain Parker of Company D did not survive the war. Many were the stories told of his concern for his men; on one occasion, in freezing weather during February 1863, he had commandeered an ambulance to bring in one of his pickets who was so frozen that he was unable to get to camp. Fires were not allowed during this tour of duty; the cold and rainy weather caused the men's clothing to freeze so that it was almost impossible for them to walk. A severe cold led to lung complications for Captain Parker, who was forced to return home to Amity and resign his command in April 1863. He died the following June.

The author of a little booklet written in 1903 for a Memorial Day observance of the Philo Paul Post of the Grand Army of the Republic spoke for anguished citizens everywhere who had been involved in the cruelest of all American wars. After the news of the dreadful Battle of Gettysburg reached Amity, he wrote, "Everything in this village stopped. The storekeepers locked their doors and went home. The shops were as quiet as death. No one was able to stem the current of sorrow."

JONATHAN LETTERMAN, MD

The Jefferson College Class of 1845 included a gifted surgeon-administrator whose achievements on behalf of medical care for battle casualties are mostly hidden away in dusty volumes about the Civil War. Yet the story of Dr. Jonathan Letterman and his accomplishments is one of the most interesting to come out of the War of the Rebellion.

Jonathan Letterman was born in Canonsburg on December 11, 1824, the son of Dr. Jonathan and Ann Ritchie Letterman. His grandfather was Craig Ritchie, a prominent Canonsburg merchant and one of the first trustees of Jefferson College, who had served with Colonel William Crawford in the Indian Wars during the 1780s. Andrew Wylie, who was at different times president of both Washington and Jefferson Colleges, was his uncle. As a youngster, tutors educated Jonathan, but he naturally attended Jefferson College, from which he was graduated in 1845. His mates described him as "one of the noblest spirits of our class." A diligent student, cheerful and hopeful, he was always prepared for class, and his friends admired his "openhearted frankness." His extracurricular activities included membership in the Philo Literary Society. Immediately after graduation from Jefferson College, Letterman entered Jefferson Medical College in Philadelphia, from which he received his degree in 1849.

The young doctor decided on a military career and was appointed almost immediately as an assistant surgeon in the United States Army. For the next twelve years, he was assigned to troop duty in the west—Kansas, Minnesota, New Mexico and California. The experience he gained in warfare against

Dr. Jonathan Letterman. Courtesy Ray W. Forquer, artist, and Countryside Prints, Inc.

the Seminoles, Utes, Apaches and Navajos came in handy during later years, for he was required to care for and transport wounded soldiers under the most primitive conditions.

When the Civil War broke out, Letterman was on duty with the Army of the Potomac. In June 1862, he was promoted to the rank of major and on

July 1 was appointed medical director of the Army of the Potomac under the command of Major General George B. McClellan.

Letterman's predecessor, Dr. Charles S. Tripler, had found problems of organization and supply somewhat overwhelming. The new director wrote that when he assumed control of the medical department, he "found it in a most deplorable condition." Officers were exhausted, medical supplies had been lost and records were in disarray. He found it necessary to completely reorganize and resupply the entire department.

Letterman's duties included the inspection of towns and villages to determine the best location for hospitals and aid stations (in addition to hospital tents, houses and barns were useful for this purpose), the securing of food as well as medical supplies and the development of a new system of records concerning patient treatment. He introduced streamlined procedures by which the wounded of both Union and Confederate armies were furnished with sufficient hospital supplies, dressings and medicines.

Through centuries of warfare, it had been the practice for fighting men to remove the wounded to aid stations behind the lines. One of Letterman's most successful innovations was the organization of a separate ambulance corps, composed of officers and enlisted men, which moved into a battle scene with two- and four-wheeled carts to remove the casualties. His

Dr. Letterman, medical director of the Army of the Potomac, with his staff, November 1862. *Courtesy* Washington Observer-Reporter.

efficient techniques for improving the field medical service by distributing hospital supplies through the chain of command network, as well as his system of evacuating the wounded by specially assigned hospital corpsmen, were procedures that were eventually adopted throughout the Union army. Modern armies all over the world have since used adaptations of his procedures.

The magnitude of the problems faced by Letterman and other medical officers is illustrated by the Civil War casualty figures. This was the most devastating of all American wars in terms of the loss of human lives. A total of 2,213,363 men served in the Union armies; of this number, 364,511 died in battle or from disease. The Confederacy suffered 133,821 deaths out of an estimated number of 600,000 to 1,500,000 servicemen. The total for both Union and Confederacy was 498,332. (World War II total of deaths from battle or disease was 407,316.) During the Civil War, a disproportionately large number of deaths from disease was the result of the rather primitive sanitary conditions that existed in the middle of the nineteenth century. The importance of antiseptics in the treatment of wounds had not yet been discovered, and many men died as a result.

Letterman did his best to improve the lot of the fighting man in the Union army, however, and the first engagement to serve as a test of his streamlined procedures was the Battle of Antietam. There, on the serene fields of late summer near Sharpsburg, Maryland, on September 17, 1862, one of the bloodiest battles of the war was fought. The combined casualties of the Northern and Southern forces that day totaled more than twenty thousand men. As he surveyed the dreadful scene, Letterman reported on the treatment of the wounded from both sides. "Humanity teaches us," he wrote, "that a wounded and prostrate foe is not then our enemy." Using his newly organized ambulance corps, he removed both Confederate and Union wounded from the field to hospital tents, private homes and barns. Many were too seriously hurt to be moved, and he found it hard to convince anxious relatives and friends that, in some instances, the recovery of the patient depended on his being allowed to rest undisturbed in the field. He was a great advocate of an abundance of fresh air in the treatment of the ill and injured. The kindness of the people in the area in opening their homes, barns (filled with hay and straw) and fields to accommodate the patients, plus a spell of good weather, helped immensely in the treatment of the casualties.

Exhausted from his labors, Letterman himself took refuge in a friendly home near the battlefield. It was there that he met Mary Lee, who became his wife in October 1863. His next assignment was that of inspector of

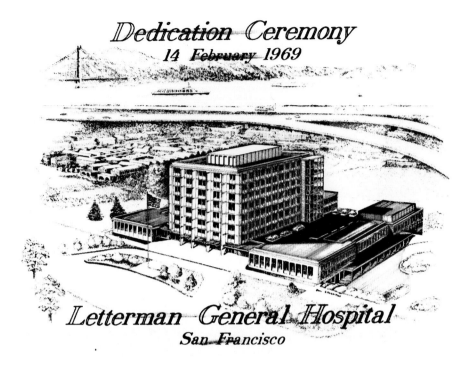

Dedication Ceremony
14 February 1969

Letterman General Hospital
San Francisco

Letterman General Hospital, San Francisco. *Courtesy* Washington Observer-Reporter.

hospitals in the Susquehanna region. After this tour of duty, Letterman resigned his commission in December 1864 and moved to California. He spent some time in the mining regions in the southern part of the state and then settled down to practice medicine in San Francisco. There, his wife died in November 1867, leaving him with two small daughters. In frail health himself, and deeply distressed and depressed by his wife's death, Letterman died on March 15, 1872.

In November 1911, the United States Army honored the man who had revolutionized the system for care of the wounded by naming its hospital at the Presidio in San Francisco the Letterman General Hospital. Established near the spectacular Golden Gate in 1898, just in time to care for Spanish-American War casualties, Letterman Hospital by World War I had become the largest military hospital in the country. In 1919, its bed capacity was 2,200; by the end of World War II, it had 3,500 beds in operation.

Letterman General Hospital served the nation well through five wars and many decades of peace, and in 1969, it dedicated a brand new ten-story high-rise building that dominated the San Francisco skyline. A staff of 1,800 carried on a modern mission, similar to that which was entrusted to Major Letterman of Canonsburg in June 1862: the duty of caring for "the health, the comfort, and the lives of thousands of our fellow soldiers who are fighting for the maintenance of our liberties." The devoted staff faithfully carried out this mission until 1995, when the Base Closure Act shut down Letterman U.S. Army Hospital after nearly a century of service to the nation.

Rebecca Harding Davis

Rebecca Harding Davis, a well-known nineteenth-century American writer of realistic fiction, was a native of Washington, Pennsylvania. Her maternal grandparents were members of pioneer families from Revolutionary War days. Her grandmother, Rachel Leet, was the daughter of Isaac Leet, who came to western Pennsylvania from Prince William County, Virginia, in 1779. In January 1807, he settled on a tract of land in Franklin Township known as Leet's Fancy. A spread of 351 acres, it adjoined a plot owned by David Hoge. Rachel Leet grew up and married Hugh Wilson, a son of James Wilson, who came to Washington from Bedford County in 1781. James Wilson built at least two houses on Main Street, one at the corner of Beau and another near Maiden in which Dr. John J. LeMoyne opened his first drugstore.

Hugh Wilson inherited various properties from his father and purchased more of his own. A successful merchant, he settled his family on an English-style country estate known as Locust Hill. He and Rachel, his first wife, had five children, two of whom are important to the story of Rebecca Harding Davis. One of the Wilson daughters, Rebecca, married James Blaine, who operated a dry goods business. It was he who bought the fine stone house built by David Bradford, after that fugitive from the Whiskey Rebellion fled to exile in Louisiana. Mr. and Mrs. Blaine, who were childless, lived and died in the Bradford House.

Another Wilson daughter, Rachel, fell in love at a very tender age with a young Englishman named Richard Harding, who came to America by way of Ireland and somehow found himself in Little Washington about 1821, looking for a place to settle down. Rachel was only about thirteen years old; understandably, Harding, twelve years her senior, was not regarded by Hugh Wilson as an acceptable suitor for his daughter. Harding went off to Alabama to seek his fortune, promising to return one day when Rachel had grown up. He established himself on a plantation at Big Spring (now Huntsville). True to his promise, he returned to Washington nine years later to claim his bride. Since Rachel's father had not changed his mind about the match, the couple eloped in August 1830 and went to Alabama to live.

Nineteenth-century author Rebecca Harding Davis. *Courtesy Rachel Loden, great-grandniece of Davis.*

Young Mrs. Harding was apparently not very happy with plantation life, and she found it hard to make friends in the tiny village. The following year, she journeyed back to Washington to stay with her sister, Mrs. Blaine, and await the birth of her first child. Thus Rebecca Blaine Harding, the future author, was born on June 24, 1831, in one of Washington's most famous landmarks, the Bradford House.

Mother and daughter returned to Alabama to live, but within five years, the family moved to Wheeling, then part of Virginia. Apparently, Richard Harding concluded that he, too, was not suited to plantation life, and his wife still yearned to be nearer her family in western Pennsylvania. In Wheeling, Harding became a successful businessman, director of an insurance company and city treasurer. By this time, the family included five children, whose education was supervised at home with private tutors.

Wheeling on the National Pike was a crossroads of America during the 1830s and 1840s. Young Rebecca and her brothers and sisters watched with awe as the vast drama of people on the move unfolded before their very eyes. Wagons loaded with merchandise, stagecoaches loaded with passengers, Conestogas packed with settlers and possessions headed west, Indians and other travelers on the go—all fascinated Rebecca and her friends. And then there was the mighty Ohio, on which they witnessed the equally splendid panorama of steamboats and other river craft transporting people and goods up and down from Pittsburgh to St. Louis on the Mississippi and thence to

New Orleans. Rebecca also became acutely aware of the grim realities of life in a booming iron-mill town, with its population of about thirteen thousand.

At the age of fourteen, Rebecca was sent by her parents back to Little Washington to attend the Female Seminary. The school, which had been in operation for nine years, was presided over by its capable principal, Sarah Foster. Rebecca's academic experience there was apparently not terribly demanding; she described the school as offering little of substance beyond religion and "soft attractive graces," plus "enough math to do accounts, enough astronomy to point out constellations, a little music and drawing, and French, history, literature at discretion." In later years, Rebecca's harsh evaluation apparently mellowed somewhat, for when Sarah Foster Hanna retired in 1874 after thirty-four years as principal, Mrs. Davis, by then an established author of many years standing, wrote in the *New York Tribune* a very appealing account of Mrs. Hanna and her lifelong efforts toward "unveiling the hidden intellect" of women during a period in history when they were expected to restrict their studies to those necessary to prepare themselves for the schoolroom or the needle.

Thus while Rebecca's experiences at the seminary may not have been as intellectually stimulating as she had hoped, she did study industriously enough to graduate in 1848 as valedictorian of her class. She also had the opportunity to attend lectures by prominent persons of the day, such as

Washington Female Seminary, line drawing. *Courtesy Citizens Library.*

Sarah Foster Hanna, redoubtable headmistress, who greatly influenced Rebecca Harding Davis. *Courtesy Washington County Historical Society.*

Horace Greeley, and to visit frequently with Dr. Francis J. LeMoyne, whom she described as "the truest representative of the radical Abolitionist in the country." Dr. Lemoyne made such an impression on the young student that, many years later, she used him as a model for an important central character in her novel entitled *Margret Howth: A Story of Today.*

During the twelve years following her graduation from the seminary, Rebecca lived with her family in Wheeling. There she helped her mother with the numerous domestic chores involved in operating a large household. And she also began to write. In January 1861, with the Civil War about to break out on all sides, the thirty-year-old Rebecca sent her first serious literary work, "Life in the Iron Mills," off to the *Atlantic Monthly*. There it was received by its editor, James T. Fields, with great joy and published in the April 1861 issue of the magazine. The short story about the wretched life of ironworkers in a mill town had such an atmosphere of grim reality and pathos that the promising author received instant and nationwide attention. The following year, she was invited by the editor of the *Atlantic Monthly* to visit Boston. This she did and within a dizzying fortnight met most of the important literary figures of the day, including the Alcotts, Nathaniel Hawthorne, Oliver Wendell Holmes and Ralph Waldo Emerson.

Escorted by her brother Wilson, she also stopped off in Philadelphia to meet a young man who had written her a fan letter after the publication of her first work in the *Atlantic*. Their correspondence had grown increasingly voluminous and friendly. The friendship soon blossomed into romance, and L. Clarke Davis proposed marriage. She accepted, and the wedding took place on March 4, 1863. The couple settled in Philadelphia, where Clarke Davis became a prominent publisher. Throughout her long life, Mrs. Davis continued to write short stories and popular novels. As time went by, their home became the gathering place for a stimulating array of writers, actors, statesmen and other important people in public life.

Into this sophisticated atmosphere of literary activity and conviviality were born a daughter and two sons. It was on her favorite and oldest child, Richard Harding Davis, that his mother lavished most of her care and attention. A handsome man and a capable writer, he became at the turn of the century one of the most dashing and popular foreign correspondents and novelists of his day. He traveled widely, and wherever he went, he seldom neglected to send home a daily note to his mother. The remarkable Rebecca, who died in 1910, and her celebrated son Richard, who died in 1916, had a sensational but brief effect on the literary tastes of two generations of Americans. And it all began in Washington, Pennsylvania.

Oil: Our Lucrative Nuisance

Life in Washington County took on an increasingly exciting quality during the 1880s when gas and oil fever broke out to a virulent degree. The coal-mining boom was no sooner underway than drilling for natural gas and oil went forward at a hectic pace.

The presence of gas in the region had been detected as early as the 1770s (yes, George Washington knew about that too), and oil had been discovered about 1821. In the early days before the Civil War, both substances tended to turn up as nuisances when drillers were boring for salt, of all things. This is how it all began.

First, it would probably be a good idea to recall how these three natural resources—salt, gas and oil, happened to be present in the first place. Like that other very desirable commodity—coal—they were the products of eons of changes and shifts in the earth's surface as plant and animal life were alternately submerged by the sea and then released by the receding waters.

Chemical reactions took place between the various elements present in the seawater and the earth itself, plus the bacteria that affected the plant life. Layers of coal, sand, gas, oil and salt were formed in great abundance in this part of Pennsylvania.

The early settlers in the region were, of course, very much in need of salt. It was in August 1821, on Little Chartiers Creek near Houston, that two men who were busily engaged in drilling for this precious substance became aware of the presence of "large quantities of fluid, or what is called gas."

The fumes that issued from the mouth of the excavation were collected in tubes and burned at night with a most "brilliant appearance." Observed the writer for the *Reporter*: "When standing on the plank over the cistern, the rumbling sound and the tremor of the timber laid over the well is distinctly felt, and perceived when the gas is coming up…the noise and agitation of the water exhibit a sight awfully sublime." Legend has it that gas escaped from this well for many years and that resourceful residents in the area used it to heat water.

Until after the Civil War, there was very little interest in natural gas. While its presence was known, it was regarded mostly as a curiosity. From time to time, children playing in the outskirts of Washington or swimming in Chartiers Creek would come across bubbling patches of gas. They then proceeded to add to the already numerous hazards of frontier life by applying a match to the escaping vapors and enjoying enormously the resulting conflagration. After the Civil War, there were occasional discoveries of gas escaping from creek bottoms and sometimes wells were dug, but nothing much came of these early explorations.

It was not until the 1880s that drilling operations began in earnest. There were twelve principal areas of exploration, identified as "sands" (beds of sandstone). The most popular were the Gordon sand in the Washington-Taylorstown area and the Buffalo, Salt, Gantz, Fourth and Fifth sands. At Prosperity, gas was obtained from the Hurry-Up sand. Numerous farms had gas deposits, and wells were drilled on many of them, including the Morgan, Willetts, Davis, Taylor, Barre, Smith, Manifold, Munce, Cameron, Thoms, Wright, Linn, Rooney, Martin, Wade, Kuntz and LeMoyne farms. Gas wells dotted the Amity field near Lone Pine as well as the banks of the Monongahela River.

Two companies heavily involved in drilling operations during the '80s were the Manufacturers Light and Heat Company and the Peoples Light and Heat Company. The latter had a particularly successful strike in April 1884 within a mile of the Washington County Courthouse, where gas was discovered at a depth of 2,068 feet on the Hess farm. This resulted in the piping of gas into Washington, where customers were charged one dollar per month for a cooking stove and seventy-five cents for each additional fire. Soon the streets of the county seat basked nightly in the warm glow of gaslights. During these early days, gas was used for heating homes, in workshops for the generation of steam, in metallurgical operations and as a source of light, especially after the development of the popular Welsbach mantle.

Gas engines were a most economical source of power in factories and oil fields, where their use resulted in a 40 to 50 percent saving over steam-powered engines. Even so, it took awhile for people to learn how to cope with this powerful and valuable new resource. Until its worth was really understood, untold quantities of gas were wasted.

Between 1883 and 1889, when the new source of energy was introduced extensively, it was used in a most "reckless and extravagant manner." Large quantities were allowed to escape from the mouths of hundreds of standing pipes. From the way that these untended pipes spewed gas, it was a wonder that the county escaped being blasted into oblivion in one giant explosion.

A few mishaps did occur. In Washington, on December 21, 1884, there was a tremendous explosion at the southeast corner of Maiden and Main when the Koechline house blew up. It seems that a lamp had been used to locate a gas leak. Another small disaster occurred on South Street when a leak in a rubber hose caused an explosion in which the side of a house was blown out. In Canonsburg, an explosion in December 1885 caused a fire that destroyed the Greer house. Fortunately, the family got out safely.

And then there was the famous McGugin well. It was in March 1882 that gas was struck at 2,200 feet on the McGugin farm near Hickory. As historian Earle Forrest put it, there was no doubt that "one of nature's marvels had been uncorked." The roar of the escaping gas was heard for miles, and all efforts to check the flow were unsuccessful. The well caught fire and continued to burn for years, night and day. Referred to at the time as "the largest flow of gas in the world," the McGugin well became quite a tourist attraction. Picnics and parties were held within the ten-mile range of its light as sightseers came from miles around to behold the startling phenomenon. In February 1886, another well was drilled near the McGugin; this slowed the flow of gas from the original well, and the energy from both was piped to Pittsburgh.

In much the same way that natural gas interfered with early drilling operations for salt, so did petroleum begin to appear and create problems in gas exploration. After Drake's discovery of oil near Titusville in 1859, interest in petroleum spread to Washington County, and an oil boomlet was under way. The first oil well drilled in the county was in 1861 when the Eureka Oil Company sank one on John Johnson's property near Amity. However, this nine-hundred-foot well was soon abandoned, along with others that had been drilled at Prosperity and Lone Pine.

It was not until the mid-'80s that successful operations got underway. In 1884, a well drilled on the Gantz property near Washington struck oil at

A county oil gusher spouts flowing gold over the derrick in Taylorstown, 1903. *Courtesy Washington and Jefferson College.*

2,191 feet, and in no time, Washington was awash with oil scouts, operators, speculators and agents. Farmers usually got one-eighth of the proceeds from oil discovered on their property, and derricks were going up all over the place. By May 1886, production reached 4,000 barrels a day. In June, it was

Oil derricks dot the landscape in Finleyville, 1903. *Courtesy Washington and Jefferson College.*

10,120 barrels, and by October, the figure was 17,549 barrels daily. Needless to say, this was a frenzied period. Fortunes were made and lost at a great rate; some wells were drilled and never completed as inexperienced operators ran into trouble at the 500- or 600-foot level, where layers of soft red sand brought drilling to a standstill.

Washington soon became a vast oil camp. One observer atop the LeMoyne well on Prospect Avenue counted more than one hundred derricks clustered at the southern edge of town, including one at the foot of Lincoln Street. Many wells were so close to private homes that the residents could step from their porches to the floor of a derrick with ease. The previously tranquil night air was disturbed by noisy sledges and anvils, as well as the monotonous puffing of steam and gas engines.

Operations in the McDonald area were particularly successful. In one three-year period during the nineties, production totaled 22,094,320 barrels with a value of $13,213,975. Other highly productive fields were located at Murdocksville, Burgettstown, Cross Creek and Cherry Valley. The hectic oil boom died down about the turn of the century as Washington County production declined, but for a wild period of about twenty years, oil and gas fever ran high in southwestern Pennsylvania.

County Draws Early Industry

It was C.N. Brady who observed in the 1880s that Washington County, because of its "healthy atmosphere, central location, and cheap fuel," would be a desirable spot to locate a glass plant.

Thus it was that one of the county's most durable industries got under way in 1887 with the organization of the first glass company to come to Washington. Known originally as Brady and Tallman, the firm soon changed its name to the Hazel Glass Company.

By 1894, the Atlas Glass Company had also begun operation, and by the turn of the century, the Hazel and Atlas companies had merged. With three plants and 1,300 employees, the Hazel-Atlas Glass Company in 1907 had a payroll of $625,000 and was the number one manufacturing concern in Washington. The three plants produced bottles and jars for chemists, druggists and food processors, as well as containers for bottling pickles, milk and ink. Hazel-Atlas canning jars, ranging in capacity from twelve to sixty-four ounces, were sold throughout the world and soon established an international reputation for the firm.

Other important glass manufacturers during the period included the Washington Glass Company that was organized in 1888 to manufacture small medicine bottles. Reorganized in 1896, the company went into the production of plain and decorated lamps, shades, globes, chimneys and novelties. The firm was eventually sold in 1900 to the Phoenix Glass Works, a branch of a large company that also had plants in Rochester and Monaca. This company, which went out of business after a few years, specialized in the manufacture of electric light supplies (excluding bulbs) that were distributed throughout the world.

Two other glass companies that were organized in 1901 remained in business for a number of years. The Highland Glass Company manufactured high quality cathedral glass and other fine products; it merged with the Mississippi Glass Company during the 1930s. And then there was the Pittsburgh Window Glass Company that enjoyed a brisk business locally for many years.

One of the most famous glass companies in the United States was very much a part of the Washington scene for more than half a century. It was after a disastrous fire had destroyed its Pittsburgh facilities in 1892 that the Duncan and Miller Glass Company moved its plant to Little Washington. The firm decided to take advantage of the abundant and economical natural gas fuel available in the area.

The partnership between George Duncan and the gifted German-born designer J. Ernest Miller had been formed in 1874. It was during the

Duncan and Miller Glass Factory. Courtesy Ray W. Forquer, artist, and Countryside Prints, Inc.

following year, when the George Duncan and Sons Glass Company was preparing designs to enter in its exhibit at the Philadelphia Centennial Exposition in 1876, that Miller created his famous "three faces" design, using his wife's profile as a model. The winning design was used for the first time on the stem of a cake plate, and it took first prize at the Centennial Exposition. The popular three faces motif was then used on other stemmed glass pieces—compotes and goblets—as well as on pitchers, fruit dishes, sugar bowls and jelly dishes. Reproductions of this world-famous design are still very desirable collectors' items.

Other famous designs created by Miller included the lovely Teardrop, delicate and lacy Young Love and the elegant Canterbury patterns. Collectors' items now, these pieces were once produced at the Duncan and Miller plant on Jefferson Avenue. When J. Ernest Miller moved to Washington with his family in December 1894, he bought the handsome Harrison Shirls home on Jefferson Avenue. While Miller retired in 1926, he never really gave up the designing work he loved so much, for he continued to go to the plant regularly until his death in January 1930. The following August, Mrs. Miller sold the family home to the Washington School District, and soon the new high school was erected on the site.

The Duncan Company continued to flourish under the direction of James E. Duncan Sr., who took over as president after his father died in 1877. (The Duncan house, built on East Wheeling Street during the 1890s, is now the home of the president of W&J College.) After Duncan Sr. died in 1900, his brother succeeded him as president, and Harry B. Duncan and the firm were incorporated as the Duncan and Miller Glass Company. It continued to produce fine glassware until 1957, when it became a division of the United States Glass Company. Unfortunately, the local factory was destroyed by fire shortly after the sale was completed.

It was also at the end of the nineteenth century that industries engaged in various forms of the iron business decided that Washington County was a good place to locate. One of the first to set up shop was the Tyler Tube and Pipe Company, organized in 1890 with a capital stock of $200,000. By 1907, it was the second-largest employer in Washington, with 760 employees and a payroll of $500,000. Originally located in New England, the firm was moved to Washington County because of all that wonderful and cheap natural gas. Tyler Tube built both rolling and tube mills, and one of its most important customers was the U.S. government, to which it sold material used in the construction of marine boilers. The guiding hand behind this enterprise was Colonel William P. Tyler who, after settling down in Washington,

Above: Eleanor Hitchcock creates etched design by painting wares with hot wax. *Courtesy Duncan and Miller Glass Museum.*

Below: Calvin Allen, one of the original workers, started at the plant in 1893. *Courtesy Duncan and Miller Glass Museum.*

became prominent in local affairs for many years. He was so influential that, after his death, the Washington Borough Council, in January 1904, passed a resolution declaring that the Seventh Ward, in which the village of Tylerdale as well as the Tyler Tube and Pipe Company were located, would henceforth be known as the "Tyler Ward." All that remains of the once important plant is the imposing office building on Jefferson Avenue that was purchased by Judge James I. Brownson in the 1930s as the headquarters for the Neighborhood House Association.

Three other turn-of-the-century industrial plants were of some interest. The production of roofing tin (thin sheets of iron coated with a tin alloy) was growing rapidly during this period. Until the end of the century, most of the market was controlled by Welsh manufacturers. Then along came two firms located in Little Washington that were among the first mills in the country to make tin plate from charcoal iron. One was the McClure Tin Mill, founded in 1897 and originally known as the Washington Tin Plate Mill. Its very modern and up-to-date plant employed 290 people with a payroll of $170,000. The company specialized in the manufacture of "charcoal iron redipped roofing plates and terne plates."

The Griffiths Tin Mill, incorporated in November 1901, also was alleged to turn out a "superior" grade of roofing tin, manufactured with a pure charcoal iron base. The president of the company, W.H. Griffiths, was well known throughout the country as one of the best tin makers of his day.

It was also just after the turn of the century, in 1901, that William Jessop and Sons of Sheffield, England, a firm founded in 1784, decided to build a plant in the United States to introduce its products to a growing American market. Again, the presence of vast coal, oil and gas deposits was a factor in the decision to build a plant in Washington County. Incorporated under the laws of Pennsylvania and operated independently of the parent firm, the Jessop plant began operations with a capital stock of $250,000. It manufactured saws, plows, shovels and other small implements, and in 1907 employed some three hundred people with an annual payroll of $208,000. Owned by American interests since 1924, the Jessop Steel Company is still in operation today as part of Allegheny Ludlum.

So the vision of C.N. Brady, who saw great industrial possibilities for Washington County more than a century ago, was more than justified. The early glass and tin plate firms have been joined by dozens of manufacturing concerns, which produce an astonishing variety of products from tin to stainless steel, glass to plastics, as well as paints,

Canonsburg Steel and Iron Works. *Courtesy Washington County Historical Society.*

bricks, clothing, ceramics, paper, rubber, electrical equipment and industrial and oil field machinery. And it all began with the discovery and development of those three marvelous sources of energy—gas, oil and coal—that transformed Washington County from a quiet agricultural region to a bustling manufacturing center.

COUNTY STEAMS INTO THE
MACHINE AGE

It is yet another of those interesting footnotes to local history that some of the earliest efforts of the Baltimore and Ohio (B&O) Railroad to build a line through Pennsylvania were carried out in Washington County. In addition, one of the most commanding figures in the early history of American railroading was Jonathan Knight, a civil engineer from Centerville, who served for twelve years as the first chief engineer of the B&O.

The Pennsylvania legislature, by an act passed on February 27, 1828, authorized the company to begin construction of a railroad in the commonwealth. Within two years, the headlong rush for railroad construction was on in earnest, and the age of machine transportation was under way in the United States. Roads on rails were nothing new—in sixteenth-century Europe, horse-drawn coaches were pulled along rails because ordinary roads were so poorly designed and maintained. So it was not surprising that the B&O, the earliest common carrier of record in the United States, first planned to build a road consisting of tracks over which coaches would be drawn by horses.

Bankers and merchants, who had very little know-how in the business of railroad construction, had organized the B&O in 1827. Of course, the whole industry was in its infancy, and the B&O, like other early companies, sent its engineers abroad to find out how the English were doing things. The only school of engineering in existence in the United States at the time was at the U.S. Military Academy at West Point. The B&O builders assumed that the base for a good railroad bed would probably be the same as that for a well-constructed highway like the National Road. Thus they turned to Jonathan Knight, the prominent civil engineer who had worked on that project. Knight was well known in Washington County; he had also surveyed and laid out the plat for Beallsville in 1821. In November 1828, the president of the B&O sent Knight and two others to England to study railroad construction.

Early B&O plans called for a line to be built from Baltimore to the Ohio River with Wheeling as the western terminus. It was to make use of coaches drawn on rails by horses. Relay stations for changing teams were to be established every 6 miles. The project would thus require at least sixty-four stations along the proposed 379 miles of track. And, of course, extra horses would be required at relay stations in the mountains. This plan of operation obviously had a number of very practical drawbacks.

Fortunately for the B&O, English and American investors were at that very moment busily experimenting with steam-driven locomotives. The record of success for the contraptions was somewhat checkered, but they looked a lot more promising than the clumsy system devised for horse-drawn trains.

At this critical moment, Peter Cooper, the inventive genius from New York, entered the picture. In August 1830, his diminutive locomotive, Tom Thumb, ran successfully on the B&O's tracks from Baltimore to Ellicott's Mills, Maryland. It lost a race with a stagecoach driver (who might well have been Lucius Stockton himself) because a fan belt slipped from a pulley, and the stagecoach reached the goal line before Cooper's little engine could get up another good head of steam. Nevertheless, it was clear that the steam locomotive was the answer for the source of power needed by the B&O to get its railroad line into operation.

Unfortunately, all this delay in locomotive experimentation proved costly to the B&O and eventually caused it to lose its original charter to operate in Pennsylvania. The 1828 charter called for construction to be completed within fifteen years. With the enormous problems involved in pioneer railroad construction, this was all too brief a period. Along with trying to resolve the power problem, engineers had to explore possible routes, another time-consuming project that required seven to eight years.

In Washington County, the route called for tracks to cross the Monongahela at Brownsville, follow Ten Mile Creek to its head and then proceed along Wheeling Creek to the Ohio River at Wheeling. A branch would cut off at the Monongahela crossing and go to Pittsburgh. After the route had been determined, the next step was to contact several hundred landowners and acquire the right-of-way.

These preliminaries took so long that the B&O applied for a four-year extension to its original charter. The request was granted by the legislature, and the B&O then had until February 27, 1847, to complete its project. However, by 1844, the road had not even entered Pennsylvania; it had been constructed only as far as Cumberland, Maryland. A second extension was clearly necessary. This time, there was considerable opposition to the B&O in both Allegheny and Washington Counties.

In Allegheny County, there was by then a great deal of interest in the Pennsylvania Railroad, which was just getting under way. This Philadelphia-based company, organized in 1846, planned to make Pittsburgh its western terminus instead of Wheeling. Pittsburgh businessmen were naturally more interested in the Pennsylvania operation. In Washington County, the opposition to a B&O charter extension came from a different source. Since the opening of the National Road in 1818, large segments of the county's population owed their livelihood to jobs related to the operation of the road. Tavern keepers, tollhouse operators, stage drivers, drovers, carriage makers and others by the hundreds who made their living on the road held protest meetings and let their representatives in the legislature know how they felt.

The B&O charter extension was denied; Pittsburgh won the Pennsylvania Railroad terminus. Washington County protesters achieved a brief reprieve for the National Road. However, the iron horse continued its inexorable march westward. A Pennsylvania Railroad train chuffed into Pittsburgh in May 1852. The B&O, after rerouting its line from Cumberland to Wheeling through Virginia as a result of the failure to get an extension to its Pennsylvania charter, ran its first train into Wheeling only six weeks after the Pennsylvania reached Pittsburgh. Washington County was thus not only bereft of its cherished National Road, on which traffic came to a standstill almost immediately, but it was also deprived of an important railroad link across the Alleghenies to the east.

During this same period, several railroad lines were chartered in Washington County. They were short lines, designed to cover distances between communities no farther apart than Pittsburgh and Washington or Waynesburg and Washington. Most of them failed before construction ever started. One, known as the Hempfield Railroad, was chartered in 1850 and organized in 1851. It was to build a line from Greensburg to Washington by way of West Newton and continue to Wheeling. Its first president was T.M.T. McKennan, and its directors included C.M. Reed, A.W. Acheson and William McKennan. Jonathan Knight was retained to help select the most desirable route. The Wheeling to Washington segment of the road

Buggy and train share the landscape—not an unfamiliar sight in Washington County. Malcolm Parcell, artist. *Courtesy of Dr. E. Ronald Salvitti.*

was completed and ready for operation by the spring of 1857 at a cost of $1,434,000. Unhappily, work on the Washington–Greensburg leg had to be suspended in 1854 because of lack of money.

The road was mortgaged in 1855. In 1861, foreclosure proceedings were begun, and the road was placed in the charge of trustees. In 1871, the Supreme Court of Pennsylvania authorized the sale of the Hempfield Railroad. It was bought by John King Jr., vice-president of the B&O Railroad, for $131,000. Thus it was that more than forty years after it began operations, the B&O finally acquired a line in Washington County.

THE WAYNIE

Pride of Two Counties

For more than half a century, a busy little railroad puffed and chuffed its way through the lovely rolling hills of Washington and Greene Counties. Affectionately dubbed the "Waynie" by generations of faithful riders, the Waynesburg and Washington Railroad came into being in 1875. The idea for the construction of a narrow-gauge railroad to connect the seats of the two counties came from John M. Day, a native of Morris Township in Washington County. One day in 1874, he wrote a letter to the *Washington Reporter* in which he outlined plans for such a road, and this communication set people to talking. The thought of a little railroad for their very own stirred all kinds of interest, and before long, meetings were held and enthusiastic citizens began to plan the project.

A few diehards who feared that a train would spell economic ruin for farmers by frightening domestic animals and destroying property values were effectively silenced as the railroad enthusiasts organized and immediately proceeded to get the necessary financial backing. A preliminary meeting was held in January 1875 at which reports on possible routes were heard and studied carefully. J.G. Ritchie of Waynesburg was elected president of the new Waynesburg and Washington Narrow Gauge Railroad Company, with James Dunn, Jacob Swart, Ephraim Conger and Thomas Iams as vice-presidents. Directors included John T. Hart, S. Rinehart, H.C. Sayers, A.A. Purman, John Munnell, John D. Wood, William C. Condit and Henry Swart.

The directors proceeded to secure a charter, and by the end of the year, a contract had been let for enough ties, at twenty cents each, for the whole route. A contract for grading the entire winding length of the roadbed was acquired by John and Charles Donogue at the rate of $1,000 per mile. The 28.16-mile distance between Washington and Waynesburg had twenty-one scheduled stops: Braddock, Judge Chambers, Vankirk, Chambers Mill, McCracken, Baker, Condits Crossing, Luellen, Mount Herman, West Amity, Hackney, Ringland, Conger, Dunn, West Union, Deer Lick, Iams, Swart, Sycamore, Rees Mill and West Waynesburg. Unscheduled stops were frequently made to pick up any passenger who was energetic enough to flag down the train; the obliging engineer would stop even in the middle of a cornfield.

Construction of the diminutive three-foot track proceeded apace during 1875 and 1876. The crossties, six feet long and six inches square, were cut from timber that lined the route. A sawmill was hauled along the way for this purpose, and the ties were stacked near the right of way at various intervals and picked up by the construction train as the work proceeded. Finally, on November 15, 1877, a triumphant announcement in the *Reporter* proclaimed, "The train from Waynesburg now arrives daily at about 11 o'clock in the morning and leaves Washington at 1:30 o'clock in the afternoon."

One-way fare cost the passenger $1.20; a round-trip ticket was $2.00. Hogs rode in the freight cars at the rate of $8.00 per carload. Sheep and coal were hauled at the rate of $6.00 a car. Business was brisk from the beginning; on one December day in 1877, five carloads of hogs were unloaded in Washington.

The first engine purchased by the company was the fourteen-ton General Greene, the second was named the General Ten Mile. The first passenger coach put into operation for the first run on October 31, 1877, had a seating capacity of forty-four and was named the West Virginia. By the mid-'20s, the Waynie was operating eight passenger and two freight trains daily except Sunday, when only four passenger trains were run. The rolling stock by then included seven locomotives, 138 freight cars with forty thousand to sixty thousand pounds capacity and 13 passenger and baggage cars.

In 1878, the twenty-eight-mile trip required four hours, one of which was spent at a switch point waiting for the other train to pass. Noted the *Reporter* on January 2, "The road is as yet too crude for fast travel. The people…are not generally speaking in a hurry. They can move a little faster and far more comfortably than by the old method (stagecoach), and they are just 'pleased to death' with the change, with the idea of having a railroad of their own, with the sense of being at last able to go somewhere by the cars like other people."

In bad weather, the four-hour trip might take longer. Since no ballast was used in the track construction, even a heavy rain might cause the train to jump the track several times en route; under such conditions, a train leaving Waynesburg one morning might not arrive in Washington until evening. Snow also created hazardous travel conditions, and trains were frequently stalled by snowstorms. By far the worst encounter with the weather occurred on November 9, 1913, when the evening train, which had departed from Waynesburg at 4:12 p.m., became completely snowbound at Braddock, almost within sight of the Washington terminal.

A sharp wind and drifting snow, however, made it impossible for the sixty passengers to proceed on foot. They were all taken in by the hospitable William Courson family; there they were fed and housed for the thirty-six hours that the storm continued. A plentiful supply of pork, tea and dozens of homemade biscuits turned out by the tireless Mrs. Courson provided enough food for the refugees. In the meantime, seventy-five W&W employees toiled ceaselessly with snow shovels to open the road. Finally, on November 11 at 6:54 a.m., the snowbound train with its weary passengers aboard chuffed into the Washington station.

By 1919, the original four-hour trip had been reduced to one hour and nineteen minutes. The twenty-eight miles included 174 curves through some of the most beautiful scenery in all of Pennsylvania. At least one of the

The "Waynie" on the Waynesburg turntable, readying for a trip back to Washington. *Courtesy Cornerstone Genealogical Society.*

The W&W coming around a bend. Note the oil derrick on the right. *Courtesy Cornerstone Genealogical Society.*

curves was so sharp that the engineer was supposed to be able to shake hands with the conductor standing on the rear platform as the locomotive snaked around the bend.

While local folks might poke fun at their dear old "Dinky" or "Weak and Wobbly," outsiders did so at their peril. The story was told of two smooth-talking travelers who planned to alight as the Waynie was puffing up a steep grade, leap across the greensward between the curving tracks and board again. The engineer decided to teach them a lesson; he worked up such a great head of steam that the two sharpies were left stranded. The honor of the Waynie was saved. Throughout its fifty-four years of passenger service, the Waynie compiled an enviable safety record. No passengers were killed or even injured, and there were but two employee fatalities. One man was killed in the 1880s when he fell between two cars and another was fatally injured in the Waynesburg yard a few years later.

The W&W originally connected with the old Hempfield Railroad near the B&O station. In time, the Pennsylvania Railroad built the Chartiers Branch of the Pittsburgh, Cincinnati, Chicago and St. Louis Railroad from Carnegie to Chestnut Street; later, the Chartiers Branch was extended to Main Street, where it connected with the W&W. On March 1, 1920, the W&W became part of the Panhandle Division of the Pennsylvania Railroad system.

Tuesday, July 9, 1929, was a sad day for those who loved the old Waynie. The last passenger train to leave Waynesburg was loaded with members of the Waynesburg Kiwanis Club. The coaches were gaily decorated with flags, banners and silly little signs reading, "Like Coolidge, we won't run again," "Pray as you enter," "On hills help push," and "Don't laugh—wait."

Tragedy marred the last day. James L. Shull, who for twenty-six years had been a passenger conductor on the railroad, brought the last regular train into the Waynesburg station about half an hour before the departure of the Kiwanis special. For sentimental reasons, he declined to make the last run. As he stood talking with friends and watching the Kiwanis train pull out of the station, he suddenly dropped dead of a heart attack.

While the durable old W&W continued to haul freight until 1934, things were not quite the same. For the thousands of faithful riders who had traveled the little railroad, a certain quality of life had disappeared. Today, a few remnants of track and trestles of the once colorful Waynie remain, and one of the locomotives reposes at the Greene County Historical Society

The proud crew of the W&W. *Courtesy Cornerstone Genealogical Society.*

and Museum. Mostly, however, it lives on only in memory and legend, commemorated by bits of doggerel composed by various wags in a burst of affectionate fun. One such little verse read:

Wriggling in and wriggling out
leaves the beholder still in doubt,
whether the snake that made the track
was going south or coming back.

DR. LeMoyne's Last Hurrah

During the mid-1850s, as the United States continued to drift inexorably into civil war, Dr. LeMoyne, broken in health but not in spirit, reluctantly discontinued his medical practice. For years, he had been plagued with rheumatism; it affected him to such an extent that he was in almost constant pain. He hobbled about stiffly and only with the support of a cane. Wracked by coughing, he could find no rest in bed. Most of his sleeping was done on a wooden settee in front of the stove in his office. Nevertheless, his sense of duty and an iron will drove him to continue his responsibilities in a number of worthwhile causes. He was still a trustee of the Washington Female Seminary and Washington College, and he followed political developments with interest as the nation plunged into war.

When the Civil War was over, Dr. LeMoyne was much concerned about the welfare of the freedmen in the South. He was a member of the American Missionary Association that had been organized in 1846. This agency occupied itself throughout the war with supplying food, clothing and medical care to the freedmen. During the five-year period from July 1864 to July 1869, it provided more than $350,000 worth of clothing and supplies, plus two thousand teachers and missionaries to teach more than 130,000 students in day schools and another 260,000 in Sunday schools. The responsibilities of this group increased when, in 1869, the federal government began to phase out the Freedmen's Bureau, leaving the American Missionary Association the only surviving organization to help the freedmen at the national level.

The association soon found it necessary to circulate an urgent appeal for funds to its friends, including Dr. LeMoyne. The postwar situation was acute in Memphis, Tennessee, where the problems of food supply, housing, sanitation, crime-control, and education grew to overwhelming proportions. Dr. LeMoyne became particularly interested in educational matters and soon contributed $20,000 to be used for the reconstruction and endowment of a school for freedmen that had been destroyed during a period of upheaval and rioting in the wake of the Civil War. His concern for the institution was so great that, in spite of physical pain and inconvenience, he even journeyed

LeMoyne portrait. *Courtesy* Washington Observer-Reporter.

to Memphis to make a personal inspection of the facility. It opened in 1871 under the name LeMoyne Normal and Commercial School, with an enrollment of 110 students. Its first graduates were granted diplomas in 1876. Throughout the remaining years of his life, Dr. LeMoyne followed the affairs of the school with great interest, making several additional gifts to its endowment. It is known today as LeMoyne-Owen College.

It was during this same period that the doctor's continuing concern with matters of education led him in 1871 to give W&J College $20,000 to establish a professorship of agriculture and correlated branches (now the chair of biology); this was followed in 1879 by a second gift of $20,000 for the establishment of a chair of applied mathematics. He also vigorously encouraged the Borough of Washington to build a new town hall; if it would do so, he promised to contribute $10,000 for a community library. The terms were accepted, the town hall was built and Dr. LeMoyne followed through with his offer. He even personally helped to select the books and catalogued them himself, laboring far into the night in front of the big stove in his office. The Citizens Library was formally opened on Thursday, March 7, 1872.

Washington's greatest benefactor had been active in community affairs for more than half a century. A variety of educational, medical, agricultural,

cultural, social and political matters had demanded and received his attention. After a lifetime of involvement in lively issues, some of them quite controversial, he climaxed the list of his causes with yet one more emotional project. He had for some time been concerned about the desirability of cremation as opposed to inhumation (burial) of the dead. His convictions on the matter were so strong that he once prepared for publication a twenty-page essay setting forth his arguments in favor of cremation. The little booklet was submitted for the "candid consideration of his fellow citizens" in the hope and belief that the "truthfulness of the reform will commend it to the assent and concurrence of the public."

It was Dr. LeMoyne's opinion that inhumation was at odds with natural law, while cremation was in harmony with it; that inhumation was expensive and wasteful, while cremation was economical; and that cremation was more sanitary. He rejected the anti-cremationist position that cremation was a pagan practice as "silly and erroneous." From a social and political point of view, he felt that inhumation served to stress the differences between poor and rich as illustrated by the distinction between plain and fancy funerals. As to the emotional objections expressed by

Postcard scene depicting the crematory. *From* History of Washington County, Vol. 1.

some, he suggested that they should adopt a more rational and reasonable approach to the matter. Finally, he argued that "the result of cremation proves the original doctrine accepted by all men, that the material is the same, whether it be of the rich or of the poor, thus illustrating the great truth of the equality of man."

So Dr. LeMoyne proceeded to carry out his latest project: he drew up plans for what was to be the first crematory in the United States. It was built on his own property at the top of Gallows Hill, and its construction in 1876 created quite a sensation. The project provided endless copy for the local newspapers, and people came from miles around to watch curiously as the twenty- by thirty-foot structure took shape. Even President Grant stopped by to see it during one of his visits to Washington. The tiny building had two rooms; one served as a reception room, and the other was the furnace room.

It was ready for use by the end of 1876, and the first cremation took place on December 6. The candidate was Joseph Henry Louis, Baron de Palm, a Bavarian nobleman who had died during a visit to the United States. The event attracted national and even international attention as physicians, reporters, diplomats and other distinguished visitors descended on Washington. A public meeting was held in the town hall, where speeches were made by an assortment of people, including Dr. LeMoyne. Finally, an impressive procession accompanied the body of the baron from the LeMoyne house up the hill to the crematory. There were further rites on the hill, and Dr. George P. Hays, president of W&J, offered the prayer. Dr. LeMoyne was the center of attention as he granted interviews to the press, entertained guests at his home and received numerous requests for speeches and articles about cremation. The whole thing showed signs of getting out of control, especially when the doctor found it necessary to write a letter to the editor of the *New York Tribune*

Baron de Palm, the first person to be cremated. *From* History of Washington County, Vol. 1.

LeMoyne Crematory. *Photogravure from* The Art of Washington County.

denying emphatically that he had compelled his children "under a threat of disinheritance to pledge themselves to personal cremation."

In due time, the uproar subsided; in a sense, it was Dr. LeMoyne's last hurrah. On October 13, 1879, he was reported lying seriously ill at his residence. He died on October 14, and his family made preparations for his burial in accordance with his wishes: his body was cremated in the little building on Gallows Hill. Then the ashes of one of Washington's most interesting citizens and greatest benefactors were placed in an urn under a simple stone monument in front of the crematory. The LeMoyne spirit traveled west, however. Charlotte LeMoyne Wills shared her father's belief in cremation. Through her efforts, the first crematory west of the Missouri River was built in Los Angeles, California, in 1887.

THE MCGIFFINS

Tales from Afar

Four generations of McGiffins were important to Washington County during the eighteenth and nineteenth centuries. Nathaniel came to America from Scotland before the Revolutionary War and served on Lafayette's staff. After the war, he settled in Amwell Township, studied law and later moved to Washington, the county seat, to practice.

His son, Thomas, was an influential Washington County businessman and lawyer. But it was Thomas McGiffin's son, Norton, and his grandson, Philo Norton, who became war heroes, and for a period of fifty years, their adventures abroad provided plenty of excitement for the folks back home. The career of Norton McGiffin was long, honorable and courageous; that of his son, Philo, was short, courageous, honorable and poignant. Both left an indelible mark on Washington County history.

Born in Washington on January 23, 1824, Norton McGiffin attended the local schools and Washington College, from which he was graduated in 1841. Like his father, he studied law but was soon attracted to a military career. When the Mexican War broke out, he enlisted in December 1846 in a Pittsburgh outfit known as the Duquesne Greys. Since fewer than forty men from Washington County enlisted for service during the Mexican War, no company was raised in the county. The Duquesne Greys left Pittsburgh in January 1847 aboard the steamboat *North Carolina*, headed for New Orleans.

After spending a couple months in camp in Louisiana, they sailed for Vera Cruz in early March. Ten thousand troops under the command of General

Winfield Scott took that city on March 29. In April, Scott's forces set out to capture Mexico City; by September 1847, his army had taken several Mexican strongholds—Jalapa, Pueblo, Cherubusco, Chapultepec and, finally, Mexico City itself. Norton McGiffin was in the thick of the fight all the way. The Mexicans did not give up easily, and in October, they tried to recapture Pueblo. It was during this final battle that McGiffin became quite a hero because of his bravery in fighting off Mexicans practically single-handedly with pistol and lance, thus saving his life and that of a comrade, William C. Winebiddle of Pittsburgh.

After the war, McGiffin settled in Washington; in May 1850, he married Sarah Quail and began a career of public service. He was elected county treasurer, and when the Civil War broke out, he was serving as sheriff. Military duty called again, and he went off with the Union Army. His tour was cut short in May 1862 when he was discharged for physical disability with the rank of lieutenant colonel. After the war, the family lived for varying periods in West Virginia, Iowa and New York as well as Pennsylvania. McGiffin represented Washington County in the Pennsylvania House of Representatives for one term in 1880–82, and he was later appointed U.S. Consul at two Canadian posts, Port Rowan and Port Hope. After a long and honorable career of public service, he died in Washington on July 20, 1905, at the age of eighty-one, the last surviving Mexican War veteran in the county.

While Colonel McGiffin's life was full of excitement and adventure, his career was perhaps eclipsed by that of his son. The story of Philo Norton McGiffin was characterized by Richard Harding Davis as that of a "real soldier of fortune." Philo McGiffin was born in Little Washington on the eve of the Civil War, December 13, 1860. Educated in the local schools, he also entered W&J College. At the end of his freshman year, he was accepted for admission to the U.S. Naval Academy at Annapolis. As a midshipman, he became known more for mischievous pranks than academic achievement. Popular with his classmates, he excelled in seamanship, gunnery, navigation and leadership in numerous reckless escapades.

One memorable prank involved a pyramid of cannonballs, relics left over from the War of 1812, which had been piled temptingly at the head of the stairs in his dormitory. One warm night, McGiffin rolled the cannonballs one by one down the stairs. The barrage created a deafening racket as the missiles tore away bannisters and demolished the wooden steps. This little caper won him a stay in the prison ship.

Another misadventure involved loading six ancient Mexican War guns with gunpowder charges and setting them all off one summer night.

The resulting explosion aroused the entire garrison, broke numerous windows and landed McGiffin in the prison ship for another period of repentance.

His impetuosity was not always directed toward mischief, however; on one occasion, he rescued two children of an academy professor from their burning home. For this heroic deed, he received a commendation from the secretary of the navy.

When the impulsive young midshipman was graduated from Annapolis in 1884, somewhere near "the tail" of his class of ninety, the navy was offering just enough commissions to fill vacancies on warships; thus in McGiffin's class, only the top twelve were chosen. The remaining graduates were "turned adrift upon the uncertain seas of civil life" after four years of academic work and two years of sea duty, in what Davis called "the best naval college in the world." To make the adjustment easier, each midshipman was awarded "a sop" of $1,000 before being sent off on his own.

The disappointed McGiffin headed west; he wrote to his mother from San Francisco that he was "in first rate health and spirits…I am big enough and ugly enough to scratch along somehow and I will not starve." By April 1885, he was in China where, through the U.S. Consul, he applied to Li Hung-chang, viceroy of Chihli Province, for a commission in the Chinese navy. Appointed to the post of professor of seamanship and gunnery at the Chinese Naval College, he was paid $1,800 per year in gold and provided with completely furnished quarters. Delighted with his house, he wrote home about its long veranda, flower garden, blooming apricot trees and cupola skylight. He asked his mother to send along his professional paraphernalia, plus pictures of the family.

McGiffin always hoped that he would have a chance to return to the U.S. Navy, and he felt that this experience abroad would prove to be very valuable. (At one time, a bill was introduced in Congress to reinstate the midshipmen who had been denied their commissions, but the measure failed to pass.) So McGiffin stayed on in China. Nine years passed; he became superintendent of the Imperial Chinese Naval College at Weihaiwei, growing more influential with each passing year.

In 1894, McGiffin applied for leave, which was approved, but before he could depart for the United States, war broke out between China and Japan. He withdrew his leave request and was placed as second in command of the seven-thousand-ton battleship *Chen Yuen*. His ship was in the thick of the fight when on September 17, 1894, the Chinese fleet engaged the Japanese in the Battle of the Yalu. During the battle, which raged for hours

Above, left: Pennsylvania State Historical Marker for Philo Norton McGiffin, at the corner of Main and Beau Streets. *Courtesy Mark Marietta, photographer.*

Above, right: Philo McGiffin, as superintendent of the Chinese Naval College. *From* Real Soldiers of Fortune.

and resulted in a crushing defeat for the Chinese, McGiffin was seriously wounded. He suffered a concussion, and his eyesight was badly impaired; he never regained his health.

McGiffin resigned from the Chinese navy and returned to the States. For the next two years, he was in and out of hospitals in New York. In spite of the fact that he was in almost constant pain, he wrote regularly to his elderly parents, concerned lest they worry about him. Finally he was confined to a hospital, where doctors urged surgery in an attempt to repair some of his injuries. He wrote, "I know that I will have to have a piece about three inches square cut out of my skull…as well as my eye taken out for a couple of hours only, provided it is not mislaid, and can be found." Told that the operation could result in insanity or blindness, he spent some of his last pain-tormented hours in the preparation of an article about the Battle of the Yalu for *Century* magazine.

At last, on the morning of February 11, 1897, he asked a nurse to bring his dispatch box. After her departure, he took his service revolver from the box; minutes later, the staff rushed to his bedside upon hearing the report of a pistol.

Richard Harding Davis took it hard. With the "pain-driven body at peace," the writer lamented the tragedy of this young American, "robbed, by the parsimony of his country, of the right he had earned to serve it, and who was driven out to give his best years and his life for a strange people under a strange flag." Today, Philo Norton McGiffin lies at peace beside his father, a hero of another war, in Washington Cemetery.

THE TENTH INFANTRY IN
THE PHILIPPINES

In the spring of 1898, as the United States became involved in a war with Spain in Cuba and the Philippines, troops from Washington County played a prominent part in the conflict. In fact, the only Pennsylvania outfit to see action in the Philippines during the Spanish-American War was the Tenth Pennsylvania Volunteer Infantry, composed entirely of men from the western Pennsylvania counties of Washington, Westmoreland, Fayette, Beaver and Greene.

Shortly after President McKinley's call for volunteers in April, Governor Daniel Hastings notified the various National Guard units in Pennsylvania that they would be mobilized. The Tenth Regiment was ordered to Mount Gretna, where on May 11 and 12, the eight companies that made up the regiment were mustered into federal service. They included Company A, Monongahela; Company B, New Brighton; Company C, Uniontown; Company D, Connellsville; Company E, Mt. Pleasant; Company H, Washington; Company I, Greensburg; and Company K, Waynesburg. The regiment was under the command of one of Washington County's most beloved military leaders of all time, Colonel Alexander Leroy Hawkins.

Born September 6, 1843, on the family farm situated on the border between Washington and Greene Counties, Alexander Hawkins came from a long line of distinguished military men. He attended the local schools until the age of fifteen when he was sent to George's Creek Academy in Fayette County. From there, he entered Waynesburg College

Colonel Alexander L. Hawkins, Civil War veteran and one of the best-loved officers of the Spanish-American War. *Courtesy Washington County Historical Society.*

in the spring of 1860. In August 1862, he left college to enlist as a private in Company K, Fifteenth Pennsylvania Cavalry. Advancing steadily through the noncommissioned ranks, he fought throughout the war with the Army of the Cumberland. Promoted to first lieutenant in the spring of 1864, Hawkins later served with the rank of captain as an aide to Major General Clinton B. Fisk until being mustered out of the service in January 1866.

After a two-year period in the drug business in Pittsburgh, Hawkins bought a farm in Washington County near Beallsville, where he became a dealer in livestock and wool. An interest in Republican politics led to his election as chairman of the party's Washington County organization and, in 1875, as county treasurer, a post he held for three years. After moving to Washington, Hawkins also served as burgess of the borough of East Washington. (The family home at 49 South Wade Avenue is now the property of the Current Events Club.)

Hawkins's continuing interest in military affairs led to his long association with the Pennsylvania National Guard. The local company of the Tenth Regiment was so disorganized and demoralized during the 1870s that there was talk of disbanding the unit. Hawkins was recommended as just the man to reorganize the company, and on January 1, 1877, he was sworn in as the new commander of Company H with the rank of captain. In February 1879, he was elected colonel of the regiment, a post that he held for the rest of his life.

Colonel Hawkins had unusual rapport with his men; his relations with those under his command were so cordial and mutually respectful that the Tenth Regiment soon developed into one of the strongest and most efficient military units in the state. It took part in subduing the Morewood riots in 1891 and the Homestead strike in 1892, as well as in numerous joyful ceremonial occasions, such as the inaugurations of Presidents Garfield, Cleveland and Harrison.

So it was not surprising that "Hawkins's Hayseed Regiment," commanded by the colonel the men affectionately addressed as "Pap," was eager to be off halfway around the world when President McKinley issued his call for volunteers in the spring of 1898. The colonel himself was more than ready to go; he spent several restless days at the old armory, then located in Washington on East Wheeling Street, impatiently awaiting orders to report to Mount Gretna. Finally, on Wednesday, April 26, the late historian Earle Forrest, who was then working as a messenger boy for Western Union, was entrusted with the telegram ordering the regiment to move out. Forrest never forgot the moment when he caught up with the colonel driving his buggy on East Wheeling Street and delivered the message. A mighty cheer greeted the news when word reached the troops at the armory.

For the first time since the Civil War, the streets of Washington and Monongahela were the scenes of many a tearful parting as the various companies of the Tenth Regiment departed on a beautiful spring morning. Company K from Waynesburg joined Company H in Washington, and

"Fighting Tenth" Washington County recruits pose proudly. *Courtesy Washington County Historical Society.*

Young Washington County soldier "with the 10th in Frisco," ready to sail for the Philippines. *Courtesy Washington County Historical Society.*

there was quite a procession as the two companies marched up Main Street to Chestnut and on out to the Chestnut Street Station. Police units, the Washington Military Band, the William F. Templeton and David Acheson posts of the GAR, Trinity Hall cadets, W&J students and dozens of relatives escorted them.

From Mount Gretna, the regiment was sent west to take part in the Philippines campaign. They sailed from San Francisco aboard the transport *Zealandia*, one of a fleet of four ships that included the *China*, the *Colon* and the *Senator*. In the Philippines, the "Fighting Tenth" served meritoriously at the Battle of Malate in July 1898 and entered Manila in mid-August. The peace treaty with Spain was signed on December 10, 1898, but U.S. troops remained on guard duty in anticipation of a revolt in the newly acquired Philippine Islands. An insurrection broke out in February 1899, and the Tenth Regiment was under fire until April. On July 1, it was ordered to sail for home aboard the *Senator*.

Throughout the Philippines campaign, Colonel Hawkins was in command of his regiment, and for distinguished service at the Battle of

Main Street looking south. *Courtesy Washington and Jefferson College.*

The Hawkins monument in Washington Cemetery honors this military family whose service to their country began with the Revolution. *Courtesy* Washington Observer-Reporter.

Malate, he was breveted brigadier general. His exemplary performance was all the more remarkable because the popular commander was mortally ill. Suffering from the effects of cancer and malaria, he was finally hospitalized on Corregidor on May 11. In spite of his desperate condition, he insisted on going home with his "boys" when the *Senator* sailed. On the night of July 18, just two days out of Yokohama, the colonel died. Fortunately, Lieutenant Colonel James E. Barnett, then in command of the regiment, had the foresight to obtain embalming fluid in the Japanese port; otherwise it would have been necessary to bury the colonel at sea.

With her flag at half-mast, the *Senator* steamed into San Francisco with the fallen commander and the sorrowing men of the Tenth Regiment aboard. At San Francisco, on August 5, one of the most impressive funeral processions in the city's history escorted the colonel's flag-draped casket to the train for the long journey back to Pennsylvania. When the entourage reached Chartiers Station in Little Washington, another procession accompanied the casket to the Hawkins home on South Wade Avenue. The next morning, it was taken to the rotunda of Old Main on the W&J campus, where the colonel lay in state until 4:00 p.m. The casket was then removed to a vault at the Washington Cemetery to await the return of the Tenth Regiment.

On its way home from San Francisco, the regiment first stopped in Pittsburgh, where on August 28, the men assembled in Schenley Park to hear themselves praised by President McKinley for "unselfish service" to their country and as "an example of patriotism and an inspiration to duty." So it was not until September 1 that the funeral of Colonel Hawkins was held on the W&J campus. After the services that included musical selections by a regimental band, prayers and remarks by Dr. Henry W. Temple and Dr. James D. Moffat, a long procession of officers, pallbearers, military dignitaries, the men of the Tenth Regiment and the general public escorted the casket to Washington Cemetery. In spite of a heavy rain, it was estimated that forty thousand people were present for the ceremonies.

Five years later, in June 1904, another twenty thousand people turned out to witness the dedication of the Alexander Leroy Hawkins Memorial at the south end of the Panther Hollow Bridge in Schenley Park, Pittsburgh. The scene of "pageantry and pride" gave evidence of "the patriotic fervor with which Americans responded to their war heroes." The handsome monument stands there still, a permanent tribute to one of Washington County's most illustrious military leaders.

Until It Was Over, Over There

The win-the-war effort in Washington County was carried forward on several fronts in 1917–18. There were liberty loan drives and war savings stamp campaigns. The Red Cross swung into action along with several other service agencies that operated under the banner of the United War Work Campaign. And then, of course, there was the draft board. Passage of the Selective Service Act on May 18, 1917, resulted in the establishment of draft boards all across the nation. In Washington County, Sheriff Frank W. Wickerham was appointed chairman of the board; the other two members were John C. Watson and Dr. E.M. Hazlett. The board in turn divided the county into five districts. The local board included Washington, East Washington and the adjacent townships. Local board members were Sheriff Wickerham, chairman; A.W. Clemens, secretary; and Dr. Hazlett, medical examiner. An advisory board, appointed to help with the medical examinations, included Drs. A.E. Thompson, L.D. Sargeant and David Beveridge. After these three physicians entered military service in June 1918, they were replaced by Drs. W.J. Burns, W.S. Grimm, J.A. Patterson, J.A. Maxwell and L.C. Honesty.

Three registrations, held in June 1917, June 1918 and August 1918, signed up men between the ages of twenty-one and thirty-one. A fourth registration in September 1918 was for men in the eighteen to forty-five age group. A total of 7,275 men were registered. The first draftees left Washington on September 5, 1917, and the last group departed a little

The first World War I recruits from Washington County. *Courtesy Washington County Historical Society.*

more than a year later, on September 18, 1918. A total of 1,052 men were "sent to the colors" by the board.

Other military men from Washington County saw service as part of southwestern Pennsylvania's reliable old Tenth Infantry Regiment. After being mustered out of federal service at the end of the Spanish-American War, the unit became a part of the Pennsylvania State Militia. In 1916, the Tenth was again mustered into federal service and sent to guard the border during the days of the "Mexican trouble." Washington's own Company H was under the command of Captain John Aiken.

After this brief period of duty, the men of the 10th Regiment returned home, only to be mustered again into federal service on Sunday, July 15, 1917. This time the unit was given a new name, the 110th Regiment, and it became a part of the 28th Division. Company H, still under the command of Captain Aiken, spent eight months at Camp Hancock, near Augusta, Georgia, training for overseas duty. Finally, on May 3, 1918, the division sailed for France. It was May 18 when they landed at Liverpool, and within the next few days, they crossed the English Channel to Calais.

During its year of service abroad, from May 1918 to May 1919, Company H participated in allied drives at Chateau Thierry, the Marne and in the Argonne Forest and finally took part in the campaign to capture Metz. After the armistice, the division was assigned to duty near the German border to support the Army of Occupation. The veterans finally sailed for home from St. Nazaire, arriving in the United States on May 12, 1919.

While all this was going on overseas, a number of vital wartime activities occupied Washington civilians on the home front. The board of trade (forerunner of the chamber of commerce) was engaged in several projects related to the war effort. The board's own headquarters, the Community Building, was all but turned over to various government offices, such as the food and fuel administrators, the internal revenue collector and assorted "civic war-work societies."

Probably the most important function of the board of trade was to stimulate war production in local industrial plants. Coal mining soon reached the greatest levels ever in Washington County; in 1918, production soared to more than twenty-two million tons. Dozens of local plants were engaged in war manufacturing. For instance, the Pittsburgh Window Glass Company turned out light armor plate for tractors. Tyler Tube and Pipe Company manufactured tubes for steamships and locomotive boilers, while the Griffith Charcoal Iron Mills made stoves as well as stove pipe for export to allied countries. The three Hazel-Atlas plants produced glass food containers; Jessop Steel manufactured light armor plate for tanks; the B.D. Northrup Foundry turned out car fittings, refinery supplies and glass moulds for industries engaged in war production. Other companies involved in war work included the Washington Tin Plate Company, which made condensed milk cans and food containers; the Duncan and Miller Company, which continued to manufacture glass tableware; the Capitol Paint and Varnish Company, which produced paints; the Washington Rubber Company which manufactured automobile tubes and tires; and the Beaver Refining Company, which turned out vast quantities of gasoline.

Money to carry on the war was an absolute must, and the story of the Liberty Loan campaigns in Washington was one of the most significant and inspiring aspects of the local war effort. The great national drive to provide financing for the war was highly successful in Washington. Five campaigns were held, and with the exception of the first, for which no quota was assigned, all drives were oversubscribed. Banks, realtors and insurance firms handled the first loan drive in Washington in 1917, and the total subscribed was $1,194,300. By the time the second 1917 loan drive came along, a more formal campaign plan had been worked out. The quota was $1,631,300, and the amount subscribed was $1,872.600. The third and fourth campaigns were opened with lots of fanfare, advertising and publicity, and in the case of the fourth drive, there was even a parade and pageant on Saturday, September 28, 1918. The quota for the third campaign was $1,647,100; it resulted in subscriptions of $1,934,150; the fourth campaign quota was $3,261,713, and the amount raised was $4,099,250. The fifth drive, described as the Victory Campaign, had a quota of $2,335,950; this, too, was oversubscribed when a total of $2,476,550 was reached.

A number of social service agencies also performed valuable war work. The Washington County chapter of the American Red Cross was organized on April 6, 1917, under the chairmanship of J.R. McCreight. Quarters to house the agency were provided by the Citizens National Bank, and soon the Red Cross had a number of projects under way. These included the inevitable but necessary fund drives, the establishment of a bureau to help soldiers' families and the preparation of bandages. The ladies were especially active. They prepared a total of five hundred thousand surgical dressings, which were shipped out by the local chapter, and busy Red Cross knitters used up twelve thousand pounds of yarn in producing some seventeen thousand knitted garments. Helmets, sweaters and wristlets were sent to each member

Victory Parade, World War I. *Courtesy Washington County Historical Society.*

of Company H at Camp Hancock, and beginning in April 1918, every departing soldier was issued a sweater, two pairs of socks and a comfort kit.

Other local organizations involved in war work included the YMCA, the YWCA, the Knights of Columbus, the Washington Lodge of B'nai B'rith, the Salvation Army and the Citizens Library. The service organizations raised funds to be used in carrying on their activities in the army and navy, while the curators of the library directed a campaign for a contribution of more than $1,000,000 to the Library War Fund. The library also rounded up more than five thousand books and magazines that were sent to libraries at Camp Lee and Camp Hancock. These agencies united in a gigantic, final fundraising effort called the United War Work Campaign. The national drive for $170,000,000 was carried on during the week beginning November 11, 1918. Washington County's quota was $350,000. The good citizens came through and exceeded the goal by $35,000.

The board of trade, along with its other activities, sponsored the War Savings Stamp campaign in 1918 and arranged for benefits to be used in providing entertainment for returning service men. And it was also the board of trade that had the honor of planning the magnificent "Welcome Home" parade and reception on September 18, 1919.

WASHINGTON READIES FOR WAR—AGAIN

The Japanese attack on Pearl Harbor on Sunday, December 7, 1941, described by President Franklin D. Roosevelt as a "date which will live in infamy," catapulted the United States into its second world war within a generation.

In Washington, Pennsylvania, an extra edition of the *Reporter* provided its readers with the grim details. In no time, as it had in every conflict since the Civil War, Washington County began to mobilize its resources to meet this new threat to the nation. On Monday, the executive committee of the Washington County Defense Council met at noon in the courthouse. Plans were made to organize, by the end of the week, every city, township and borough in the county to meet any emergency. Defense Council Headquarters, open on a twenty-four-hour basis, were immediately set up in the Sheriff's Office. In the days that followed, emergency defense council meetings were held in Canonsburg, Claysville, Charleroi, Monongahela, McDonald, Donora and North Charleroi.

Speedy measures to deal with the emergency were immediately undertaken in cities and towns throughout the nation. Uniformed soldiers appeared as if by magic to guard the famous Key Bridge in Washington, D.C.; at the same time, in Little Washington, the first order of business for Company H, Third Regiment, Pennsylvania Reserve Defense Corps, was to secure the county bridges that spanned the Monongahela River. By Tuesday, details of twelve men each had been dispatched to guard the bridges at Monongahela, Masontown and West Brownsville. The

Military formation on campus during World War II. *Courtesy Washington and Jefferson College.*

bridge at West Brownsville was a particularly important link in the modern National Pike that extended from Baltimore to Los Angeles. As U.S. Route 40, it was vital to the defense transportation network in southwestern Pennsylvania. By the end of the week, men were also sent to guard the bridge at Elizabeth, and along the Pennsylvania Turnpike, State Police, augmented by men from reserve army units, stood watch over the seven tunnels of the superhighway.

When war broke out, there were already some three hundred defense plants in western Pennsylvania that were producing $200,000,000 worth of armaments. These facilities, plus public utilities, were placed on a war footing on December 8. Acting on warnings from army, navy and FBI officials, these plants took steps immediately to increase police guards and implement anti-sabotage measures. Double guards were stationed at all plant entrances as well as at vulnerable points within the premises, and employee identification

WORLD WAR II WAR EFFORT

During World War II, Duncan and Miller Glass Company competed for and received contracts from the War Production Board in Washington, D.C. A fine job was done in making Norden Bomb Sight parts and booster adapters for rockets. More than 75 million yellow clay targets used in gunnery training were produced in western Pennsylvania for United States force. Duncan and Miller Glass products were shipped all over the world.

Duncan and Miller Glass Factory contributes to the war effort. *Courtesy Duncan and Miller Glass Museum.*

procedures were tightened. Similar protective measures were taken to secure power plants, reservoirs and pumping stations.

Pennsylvania's veteran Twenty-eighth Division was returning from maneuvers in the Carolinas when news of Pearl Harbor reached the troops. They were in bivouac near South Boston, Virginia, on their way back to Indiantown Gap. It was December 10 when the sixteen thousand men returned to their home base, praised by their commander, Major General Edward Martin, who said the troops performed "magnificently in the war games and returned in excellent condition."

Meantime, back in Little Washington, county officials worked feverishly to get the defense apparatus ready for any emergency. Representatives of fire departments, police forces and constables from all over the county met at the courthouse on December 9 to mobilize for defense. The Washington Women's Defense Council also got going as representatives from all local women's groups assembled that night in the chamber of commerce rooms to listen while William E. Barron, superintendent of Washington Hospital, outlined procedures for organizing volunteers to serve in various civil defense activities. In less than a week, the ladies began a house-to-house canvas to register men and women for volunteer defense work.

One of the first wartime regulations to jolt the public went into effect on December 10, when the Office of Price Mobilization (OPM) issued an order to prohibit, for a twelve-day period, the sale, either wholesale or retail, of automobile tires and tubes. The restriction did not apply to retreads, used tires or tubes or to tires and tubes on new or used vehicles. The measure was taken to head off a consumers' buying spree that developed as motorists decided to stock up on potentially scarce rubber tires and tubes.

War or no war, community life went on. Numerous scheduled events took place during the week following the declaration of war against Japan on

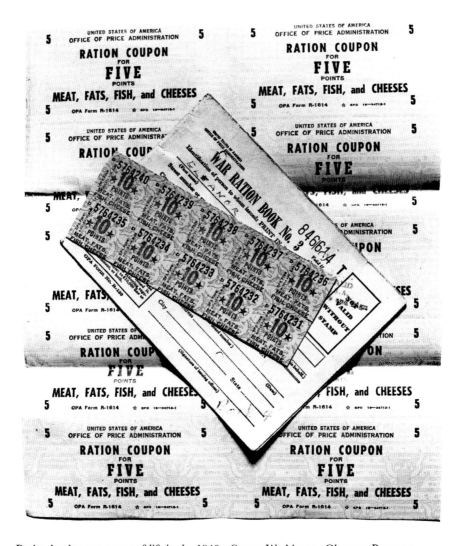

Ration books were a way of life in the 1940s. *Courtesy* Washington Observer-Reporter.

December 8. Members of the January class of Washington High School presented the annual senior play, *The Kid*, in the high school auditorium. At the YWCA, another annual event, the Old World Market, took place as scheduled. It featured craft displays, a program of international dances and a tea and style show from countries all over the world.

Other items from a busy week: members of the Current Events Club agreed that they would sponsor a Red Cross knitting unit; the students of the

Washington Seminary held their annual first-semester dance on December 12 in the Oval Room at the George Washington Hotel; the Washington School Board authorized the superintendent to use school buildings for billeting troops if necessary; plans for the annual Charity Ball, scheduled for December 29, proceeded; the members of the Trinity High School Class of 1928 held their first reunion since graduation in the Rose Grill of the William Henry Hotel, with thirty members and guests present; the army recruiting station at the post office was ordered to open seven days a week from 8:30 a.m. to 8:30 p.m.; and a World War I Russian flying ace, Major Alexander de Seversky, got a lot of attention when he came to town to speak at Washington High School as part of the Arms Club lecture series. His topic: "The Future of Air Power."

For those in search of a movie to get away from it all, the Basle offered George Brent and Bette Davis in *The Great Lie* (matinee: fifteen cents,

Service men and women in formation in front of McIlvaine Hall. *Courtesy Washington and Jefferson College.*

evening: twenty cents). At the Court, Irene Dunne and Robert Montgomery could be seen in *Unfinished Business*. And, from another war and another era, the Mary Emma McNulty Tent No. 26, Daughters of Union Veterans, held its annual election in the public meeting room of the courthouse on Friday, December 12. The president of the state organization made her annual visit at this meeting; she commended the tent for the work it was doing and asked that the group carry on during the present crisis. A special guest at the meeting was a Civil War veteran, Commander A.T. Anderson, who spoke briefly on the current world situation.

Then there was the twenty-one-year-old truck driver in Greensburg who apparently did not appreciate the seriousness of the national crisis. He was handed a thirty-day jail term for making insulting remarks to two sentinels guarding a bridge at New Kensington.

By mid-week, America was at war with Italy and Germany as well as Japan, and the American Red Cross launched a national drive for $50,000,000. The Washington County quota was set at $70,000; plans were made to kick off the local campaign on January 5, 1942. Conscious of the fact that most citizens were eager to help in the war effort, an editorial writer for the *Reporter* analyzed the situation and assessed the job to be done in the years ahead: "Now that the guns are roaring and the planes are flying is the time for all Americans worthy of the name to rally behind the President… confidence and national unity are two factors which must be attained…the whole energy of the people must be devoted to the single purpose before us."

BIBLIOGRAPHY

Alberta, R.C. *Mount Washington Tavern*. Fort Washington, PA: Eastern National Park and Monument Association, 1971.

Baldwin, Leland D. *Whiskey Rebels*. Pittsburgh, PA: University of Pittsburgh Press, 1939.

Brignano, Mary. *The People's Palace 1900–2000*. Pittsburgh, PA: Broudy Printing Co., 2000.

Buck, Solon J. *The Planting of Civilization in Western Pennsylvania*. Pittsburgh, PA: University of Pittsburgh Press, 1939.

Carnegie Magazine, Summer 1979. Pittsburgh, PA.

Coleman, Helen. *Banners in the Wilderness*. Pittsburgh, PA: University of Pittsburgh Press, 1956.

Commemorative and Biographical Record of Washington County, PA. Chicago: J.H. Beers and Co., 1893.

Creigh, Alfred. *History of Washington County from Its First Settlement to the Present Time*. Harrisburg, PA: B. Singerly, Printer, 1871.

Crumrine, Boyd. *Art Work of Washington County (Published in Nine Parts)*. Chicago: Gravure Illustration Company, 1905.

———. *Courts of Justice, Bench and Bar of Washington County, PA*. Chicago: Lakeside Press, 1902.

———. *History of Washington County*. Philadelphia, PA: L.H. Everts, 1882.

Davis, Richard Harding. *Real Soldiers of Fortune*. New York: C. Scribner's, 1911.

Dictionary of American Biography, vol. XI. New York: C. Scribner's, 1946.

Farrar, Samuel C. *Twenty-second Pennsylvania Cavalry and the Ringgold Battalion*. Pittsburgh, PA, 1911.

Forrest, Earle R. *The Duncan and Miller Glass Co.* Washington, PA: Ward Printing Co., 1957.

———. *History of Washington County, Vol. 1.* Chicago: S.J. Clarke Publishing Co., 1926.

Learned T. Bulman '48 Historic Archives & Museum. Washington & Jefferson College, Washington, PA.

McCready, Albert L., and Lawrence W.R. Sagle. *Railroads in the Days of Steam.* New York: American Heritage Publishing Co., Inc., 1960.

McCulloch, M.C. *Fearless Advocate of the Right.* Boston: Christopher Publishing House, 1941.

McFarland, J.F. *Twentieth Century History of Washington County.* Chicago: Richmond-Arnold Publishing Co., 1910.

Official History of the Operations of the Tenth Pennsylvania Infantry, U.S. Volunteers, June 1963.

Official Records of the Union and Confederate Armies. Washington, D.C.: Government Printing Office, 1887.

Pennsylvania in the Great American Conflict, Memorial Day, Amity, 1903. Washington, PA: H.F. Ward, Printer.

Photographic History of the Civil War. New York: Review of Reviews Co., 1912.

Pittsburgh Dispatch. July 10, 1898.

Reporter. August 15 to October 17, 1808; 125th anniversary issue, August 15, 1933; Sesquicentennial issue, August 15, 1958; August 23, 1980; December 7–16, 1941; and June 5–10, 1944.

Rural Reflections of Amwell Twp. Volume 2. N.p.: Bicentennial Committee of Amwell Township, 1978.

Searight, T.B. *The Old Pike.* Edited by J.E. Morese and R.D. Green. Orange, VA: Green Tree Press, 1971.

Slagle, Lawrence W. *B&O Power.* Carrollton, Ohio: Standard Printing and Publishing Co., 1964.

Stevens, S.K. *Pennsylvania, Birthplace of a Nation.* New York: Random House, 1964.

Stewart, R.L. *History of the One Hundred and Fortieth Regiment, Pennsylvania Volunteers.* N.p.: Published by Authority of the Regimental Association, 1912.

Vinacke, H.M. *A History of the Far East in Modern Times.* New York: F.S. Crofts and Co., 1946.

Washington and Jefferson College Annual 1885. Washington, PA.

Washington Sesquicentennial, Official Program. Washington, PA, 1960.

About the Author and Editors

Harriet Branton

Harriet Branton, who holds a bachelor of arts degree from George Washington University, has enjoyed a varied career. She has worked in the Library of Congress and with the Food and Agricultural Organization of United Nations in Washington, D.C. As an army lieutenant, she was commanding officer of the WAC detachment at West Point. After moving back to Pennsylvania, Mrs. Branton was a teacher and—for more than fifteen years—a freelance writer of historical

Courtesy Chevy Chase House.

features for the *Washington Observer-Reporter*. Her articles have also appeared in various alumni publications and historical journals, including the *Western Pennsylvania Historical Magazine, Allegheny Magazine, Pennsylvania Heritage* and *Country Magazine.*

Mrs. Branton, a native of Pittsburgh, Pennsylvania, lived for fifty years in "Little Washington" where her late husband, Clarence, was a professor of English at W&J College for thirty-five years. She lives in retirement in Washington, D.C., near her children and grandchildren.

EMSIE MCILVAINE PARKER AND LESLIE PARKER

Emsie McIlvaine Parker was born and raised in Washington County. Her family, on both sides, settled there in the early 1800s, and she grew up steeped in the rich local history. After undergraduate work at Oberlin College and Boston University, she held a teaching fellowship in English at the University of Pittsburgh. Leslie Parker holds a PhD in molecular biophysics and biochemistry from Yale University.

History has been a common ground for this couple. Throughout the 1980s, they looked forward to Harriet Branton's weekly newspaper articles on Washington County history. Recognizing the intrinsic value of these delightful, meticulously researched and well-crafted tales to the present generation, they determined not to allow them to be lost in time. The Parkers currently reside in Edwards, Colorado.

About the Artists

Ray W. Forquer

Ray Forquer is recognized for the popular appeal and historical accuracy of his work. During the past thirty-five years, Forquer has received praise from critics and many awards for his ability to combine glimpses of history with his native Western Pennsylvania landscapes. His landscape paintings, historical works, portraits and limited edition prints are included in an ever-growing number of corporate and private collections. Several of his paintings have been chosen to illustrate historical books dealing with the Civil War, the Whiskey Rebellion of 1794 and decisions in the presidency of George Washington. His work has also appeared in several national magazines, newspaper articles and television documentaries. Owner of Countryside Prints, Inc., he resides in Washington, Pennsylvania.

J. Howard Iams (1897–1964)

J. Howard Iams had a lifelong interest in Pennsylvania and often chose as his subjects the homes, farms and mills related to the region's history and development. The Whiskey Rebellion works are considered his most ambitious project, and he spent years researching the topic. Many of his paintings are in the Westmoreland Museum of American Art.

MALCOLM STEPHENS PARCELL (1896–1987)

Born in Claysville, Washington County, Malcolm Parcell gained a national reputation. By his mid-twenties, he had a studio in New York, received plenty of press and awards and won the coveted Saltus Gold Medal from the National Academy of Design and steady work in illustration and high society portraiture. But his inspiration was in western Pennsylvania. He returned, painting in his rural home, "Moon Lorn," until his death at ninety-one. His works are in Washington and Jefferson College, museums and distinguished private collections.

Visit us at
www.historypress.net

This title is also available as an e-book

When the Animals Saved Earth

An Eco-Fable

RETOLD BY

Alexis York Lumbard

ILLUSTRATED BY

Demi

❖ Wisdom Tales ❖

A gem of an island glimmered in the bright, blue sea. Here the winged and webbed, hoofed and horned, mighty and meek, all lived in peace.